Clair Martin

The Footmen and Horses in Our Midst

THE BATTLE FOR AMERICA
A Game of Life or Death

The Footmen and Horses in Our Midst

THE BATTLE FOR AMERICA
A Game of Life or Death

PAUL E. DONLEY

ACW Press
Ozark, AL 36360

Scripture quotations are taken from the King James Version of the Bible.

THE BATTLE FOR AMERICA,
A GAME OF LIFE OR DEATH
The Footmen and Horses in our Midst

Copyright ©2005 Paul Donley
All rights reserved

Cover Design by Alpha Advertising
Interior Design by Pine Hill Graphics

Packaged by ACW Press
1200 HWY 231 South #273
Ozark, AL 36360
www.acwpress.com
The views expressed or implied in this work do not necessarily reflect those of ACW Press. Ultimate design, content, and editorial accuracy of this work is the responsibility of the author(s).

Library of Congress Cataloging-in-Publication Data
(Provided by Cassidy Cataloguing Services, Inc.)

Donley, Paul E.

The battle for America : a game of life or death / Paul E. Donley. -- 1st ed. -- Ozark, AL : ACW Press, 2005.

 p. ; cm.
 ISBN: 1-932124-45-4
 ISBN-13: 978-1-932124-45-3

 1. Christianity--United States--21st century. 2. Christianity and politics--United States. 3. Religion and state--United States. 4. Social change--United States--Religious aspects. I. Title.

BR115.P7 D66 2004
277.3/083--dc22   0412

All rights reserved. No part of this book may be reproduced, stored in a retrieval system, or transmitted in any form or by any means—electronic, mechanical, photocopying, recording, or otherwise—without prior permission in writing from the copyright holder except as provided by USA copyright law.

Printed in the United States of America.

I Gratefully Acknowledge…

I want to humbly acknowledge my deep appreciation and thanks to all those who by the divine grace of God caused this message in book form to be written, and published. I would like to mention the people of The Open Door Church in Chambersburg, PA for their prayers and encouragements including my former pastor, Keith Skelton, and Karen Myers for taking time from her busy schedule to work on the book cover; Dr. Dino Pedrone, my former pastor for his review and kind words; the various organizations for permission to quote from their material; Carl and Mary Smith for their prayers and financial support; the publishers, America Christian Writers Press for their tremendous support and dedication in taking on a manuscript from a new author; Heather Yamamura for her professional editing and review; my wife, Marion, for her editing work and patience; and Sandra, my daughter, for her review of portions of this work.

Above all, I want to acknowledge my heavenly Father and Savior, the Lord Jesus Christ for His calling and inspiration through the Holy Spirit, without which His book could never have been written.

Paul Donley

CONTENTS

Introduction and Background 9
1. Reasons Why Satan Wants to Destroy America........ 15
2. The Means by Which Satan Is Destroying America 37
    A. The Footmen in Our Midst 37
    B. The Horses in Our Midst 48
3. The Battlefield............................ 133
4. Some Final Words 147
5. What Can We Do? 151
6. Conclusion 157

INTRODUCTION AND BACKGROUND

DEAR FRIEND, I want to thank you for choosing to purchase this book. The introduction to this book may seem unusual and surprising compared to the typical books one may read, but I trust this will be the beginning of surprises and of great encouragement for you.

We, as a nation are experiencing changes as well as unusual times across our great land. Americans are being exposed to a great departure from the once-held standards of our society. A great number of Americans, especially our young people, are confused and may not realize it, being without direction in life and without standards of conduct. This is a result of incredible deception. America seems to be out of control, as we are bombarded with all the various lifestyles and teachings imaginable. I ask you to lay aside preconceived ideas, what your friends believe or are doing, what you have been told, and say to yourself, "If there is a better way of life, I want to know about that kind of life."

I encourage and challenge you to venture into this message and allow your heart to listen to what you are about to read. I trust you will not read just certain sections of this book and disregard the rest, but read with an understanding and receptive heart *the entire book*. This is very important in order to grasp a solid understanding of the total picture of what is being revealed. I know you will read about some things that you have never before read or heard. Then there will be some things that will astound and shock you, which you may find unbelievable, but as you *continue to read*, will find believable.

I use the Bible as my main reference in presenting my argument, as I believe it to be the inspired authoritative Word of God (2 Timothy 3:16, and 2 Peter 1:21). I will illustrate throughout this book the reasons why I believe the Bible should be taken as the basis for the foundation and standard for governing a society, and a nation, and as such *is my only defense*. I make no apology for my statement. CAUTION! If you come this far and decided not to continue reading, I believe that would be a great tragedy for you because you never gave yourself a chance to experience the rest of the story. During the course of your reading, I trust you will find some things that will stir your innermost being to take action, and possibly change your life forever. This is especially true if you care about yourself and others, and have a love for our great land of America. So, that being said, let us continue and start off with the Bible, using the King James Version.

I invite you to have a Bible handy, or if not, I have given most of the Scriptures. We will begin by reading in Jeremiah 12:5, then Ezekiel 22:30-31, Psalm 9:17, and 2 Chronicles 7:14. These Scripture verses are the heart of this message to the Church, and to every person in America:

> *Jeremiah 12:5, "If thou hast run with the footmen, and they have wearied thee, then how canst thou contend with the horses? And if in the land of peace, wherein thou trustedst, they wearied thee, then how wilt thou do in the swelling of Jordan?"*

> *Ezekiel 22:30-31, "And I sought for a man among them, that should make up the hedge, and stand in the gap before me for the land, that I should not destroy it: but I found none. Therefore have I poured out mine*

Introduction and Background

indignation upon them; I have consumed them with the fire of my wrath: their own way have I recompensed upon their heads, saith the Lord God."

Psalm 9:17, "The wicked shall be turned into hell, and all nations that forget God."

2 Chronicles 7:14, "If my people which are called by my name, shall humble themselves, and pray, and seek my face, and turn from their wicked ways: then will I hear from heaven, and forgive their sins, and heal their land."

What can be more tragic and challenging than these words from the grieving heart of God to His beloved people, the nation of Israel! The stern warnings from God stemmed from the numerous times Israel and Judah had turned their backs on the goodness of God, turned again to the practice of sin and the ways of the heathen nations. During these times God raised up His messengers, or prophets, to warn the people of Israel and Judah of apostasy, and the downward spiral to disaster. Two such prophets were Jeremiah and Ezekiel. They spoke boldly, fearlessly, and without compromise. They loved the people of Israel and Judah, and spoke as patriots and revivalists in their days. Jeremiah was God's prophet to Judah, and Ezekiel to both Israel and Judah. Their message was a message of naming sins, calling for repentance, and giving warnings of coming judgment. God spoke to Israel's leaders, through His prophets, these words: *"For my people is foolish....they are wise to do evil, but to do good they have no knowledge"* (Jeremiah 4:22); *"without understanding; which have eyes, and see not; which have ears, and hear not"* (Jeremiah 5:21); *"Were they ashamed when they had committed abomination?*

nay, they were not at all ashamed, neither could they blush" (Jeremiah 6:15); *"This is a nation that obeyeth not the voice of the Lord their God, nor receiveth correction: truth is perished, and is cut off from their mouth"* (Jeremiah 7:28); *"Many pastors have destroyed my vineyard, they have trodden my portion under foot, they have made my pleasant portion a desolate wilderness"* (Jeremiah 12:10); *"They have forsaken my law which I set before them, and have not obeyed my voice, neither walked therein; but have walked after the imagination of their own heart"* (Jeremiah 9:13-14); *"Learn not the ways of the heathen"* (Jeremiah 10:2); *"Her priests have violated my law, and have profaned mine holy things: they have put no difference between the holy and profane....and I am profaned among them"* (Ezekiel 22:26).

Do these words sound familiar? If they don't they should, for this is a picture of the moral condition of our beloved America. I trust *you will reread those words of God*. In Jeremiah 12:5, God was speaking primarily to His prophet, for he became weary of warning the people of Judah about their sins and the coming judgment, but they would not listen. Therefore, God allowed a heathen nation, Assyria, to destroy and take captive Israel, the northern kingdom. Then later Judah, the southern kingdom, followed the wicked example of Israel, and ended up in captivity in Babylon.

Israel and Judah's rebellion and sinfulness brought God's wrath upon them. God allowed heathen nations to destroy and take them captive, and eventually scatter His people among all the nations of the world to this day. These warnings came true for Israel and Judah. I believe God is giving our nation the same warnings **for we are practicing the same sins, and not listening!**

With this background in mind, I want to share with you something that is close to my heart for which I have continual sorrow and a heavy burden. It is for our great land of

Introduction and Background

America. I believe *millions of lost souls as well as backsliding Christians in America are incredibly blinded and deceived by Satan and do not realize it.* This is one of the reasons God has laid upon my heart the subject: *The Battle for America, A Game of Life or Death, The Footmen and Horses in Our Midst.* Later on in the book I will share with you how and when God brought about this book and its message.

You may be asking, "What do you mean by 'The Battle for America?'" Let me say at the outset of this message that the battle I am speaking about is not a physical battle—we are not being invaded by a foreign nation, **at least not at the present time!** But, I hasten to say that a few nations at this very moment, like Communist China, are building up their armed forces and missile arsenals, using our technology and our know-how to eventually have military superiority over us—then look out America! But, America is playing politics, calling it trade agreements, and becoming willingly oblivious of this great threat.

However, *the battle I am going to talk about is spiritual.* Ephesians 6:12 says, "For we wrestle not against flesh and blood, but against principalities, against powers, against the rulers of the darkness of this world, against spiritual wickedness in high places." **We are in a gigantic spiritual warfare for our nation, beloved.** The battle is between the people of God and the people of Satan. It has always been like this throughout Bible history. God calls Satan "the god of this world" (2 Corinthians 4:4); that is, Satan is the god of this world system. Satan wants complete control over *all* people of the world, and he is using his **"system"** to do just that. His on-going system of clever deception is presented as the normal way of living since Adam and Eve, and is at work this very moment. I trust you will see this as you continue to read the rest of this book.

Satan's goal is to obliterate Christianity from this world, including the center for Christianity, namely America. I believe with all my heart that America is in the most critical stage of her existence as Satan is going all out to destroy this nation, more so than ever before in the history of this great land. It is my earnest desire that America listen to this message from my heart. This message is primarily addressed to the Church, for it is in the spotlight. But, I hasten to say that this message is to the nation I love, America. It is therefore to every person in America, for it is a message of love. I could not have written this book if I did not love the people of our great nation, and the God who created America. I trust this book will cause a stirring in your heart as God stirred my heart at this very critical hour of our nation's existence.

CHAPTER ONE

Reasons Why Satan Wants to Destroy America

LET US CONTINUE this adventure with reasons why I believe Satan wants to destroy America:

A. America Is God's Nation:

Mark it down friend, or better yet write it on your heart. And if you love America, America should be in your heart. Tell it to your children, and to your neighbors; tell it everywhere you go, and let people know that God gave birth to this nation. It was God who gave birth to the nation of Israel. God led them out of Egyptian oppression and bondage, and led them across the Red Sea into a land flowing with milk and honey. Likewise, I believe it was this same God who raised up a Christian remnant of people, led them out from under the religious oppression of the Church of England, and across a wide ocean to a land flowing with milk and honey to give birth to America. "For the Lord thy God bringeth thee into a good land, a land of brooks of water, of fountains and depths that spring out of valleys and hills" (Deuteronomy 8:7).

That small remnant of Christian people were called "The Pilgrims." It was in November 1620, that they anchored their ship the "Mayflower" off shore at what is now called Cape Cod, and later on in December they sailed across Cape Cod Bay and settled at what is now called Plymouth, Massachusetts. But before this momentous time came about in our Christian heritage, another great event took place. Let us look at the person I believe to have been the forerunner for the Pilgrims. That person has often been referred to as the one who discovered America—Christopher Columbus. In 1492, Christopher Columbus, an explorer, discovered the New World, or as Columbus called it, "the second part of the earth," a new continent that included a land now called America. The name *Christopher* means "Christ-bearer."

Columbus first set foot not on America, but an island that is now part of the Bahaman Islands. This island he "christened 'San Salvador' meaning 'Holy Saviour,'—and Prayed: 'O Lord, Almighty and Everlasting God, by Thy Holy Word Thou hast created the heaven, and the earth, and the sea; blessed and glorified be Thy Name, and praised be Thy Majesty, which hath designed to use us, Thy humble servants, that Thy Holy Name may be proclaimed in this second part of the earth.'"[1]

Again he wrote, "I conceive to be the principal wish of our most serene King, namely the conversion of these people to the holy faith of Christ....Therefore, let the King and Queen, our Princes, and their most happy kingdoms, and all the other provinces of Christendom render thanks to our Lord and Saviour Jesus Christ, who has granted us so great a victory and such prosperity....Let Christ rejoice on earth, as

He rejoices in heaven in the prospect of the salvation of the souls of so many nations hitherto lost."[2] Truly Christopher Columbus was a Christian missionary sent from God to prepare the way for the Pilgrims voyage in 1620.

The Pilgrims drew up what was called "The Mayflower Compact," which stated, "In the name of God, Amen. We whose names are underwritten, the loyal subjects of our dread sovereign lord, King James, by the grace of God, of Great Britain, France, and Ireland, King, Defender of the Faith, etc. Having undertaken for the glory of God, and advancement of the Christian faith and honor of our king and country, a voyage to plant the first colony in the northern parts of Virginia, do by these present, solemnly and mutually, in the presence of God and one another, covenant and combine ourselves together into a civil body politic, for our better ordering and preservation and furtherance of the ends aforesaid; and by virtue hereof to enact, constitute, and frame such just and equal laws, ordinances, acts, constitutions, offices from time to time as shall be thought most meet and convenient for the general good of the colony; unto which we promise all due submission and obedience. In witness whereof we have hereunder subscribed our names, Cape Cod, 11th of November, in the year of the reign of our sovereign lord, King James, of England, France, and Ireland 18, and of Scotland 54. Anno Domini 1620."[3]

William Bradford, one of the Pilgrims and the governor of the Plymouth Colony, penned these words: "Thus out of small beginnings greater things have been produced by His hand that made all things of nothing, and gives being to all things that are; and as one small candle may light a thousand, so the light here kindled hath shone unto many, yea in some sort to our whole nation; let the glorious name of Jehovah have all the praise."[4] I personally believe that the birth of our great nation began in 1620 with Governor William Bradford and the Pilgrims, the first of the line of Founding Fathers. Later on, others arrived in the line of Founding Fathers, like William Penn in 1682, who said, "The best way to make citizens good is to convert them to Christ....Liberty without obedience is confusion and obedience without liberty is slavery....people who will not be governed by God must be ruled by tyrants....Penn was the first person to propose a United States of America."[5] The state of Pennsylvania was named after Penn. In Pennsylvania is the famous Liberty Bell of 1752 with the famous inscription from the Bible that reads, "**LEV XXV:X PROCLAIM LIBERTY THROUGHOUT ALL THE LAND UNTO ALL THE INHABITANTS THEREOF.**"

In 1735 America experienced what was called the Great Awakening, with preachers like Jonathan Edwards, a Yale graduate, who "stressed the sovereignty of God, the depravity of man, and the Gospel of the grace of God." George Whitefield, from England, conducted many crusades, and thousands came to faith in Christ. As a result of the fervent ministries of these evangelists, it was said that one-sixth of the population of New England was converted to Christ in a two-year period.[6]

God raised up other great leaders among our Founding Fathers who were the framers of these great documents:

July 4, 1776, The Declaration of Independence: Thomas Jefferson, the principle author and signer became our third president. Fifty-five other signers included John Hancock, Benjamin Franklin, John Witherspoon (a minister), Samuel Adams, and John Adams. The document states, "We hold these truths to be self-evident: that all men are created equal; that they are endowed by their Creator with certain unalienable rights; among these are life, liberty, and the pursuit of happiness...."

September 17, 1787, The Constitution, and the Bill of Rights: George Washington, our first president, superintended the framing of this document,[7] and James Madison was the principle designer along with the other thirty-nine signers, including Alexander Hamilton and Benjamin Franklin. The opening words of this document read, "We the people of the United States, in order to form a more perfect union, establish justice, insure domestic tranquility, provide for the common defense, promote the general welfare, and secure the blessings of liberty to ourselves and our posterity, do ordain and establish this Constitution for the United States of America." Thus the birth of our nation was completed for the thirteen original colonies, or thirteen United States.

Our nation matured over the years to fifty United States. The name of God is on, or is implied in these great documents as well as His handiwork of inspiration. Whether the framers were Deists, or Christians, God gave birth to our nation using these people who honored Him. No other nation on the face of this earth has documents such as ours. They are unique. Dear friend, have you read these documents? If you have not, I urge you to read them soon.

In 1892 the Supreme Court declared our nation to be "a Christian nation." In 1931 Justice George Sutherland said that Americans are a "Christian people." And in 1952, Justice William O. Douglas said, "We are a religious people and our institutions presuppose a Supreme Being."[8]

Recently, one Christian writer boldly said, "America is certainly not God's nation." Really! If America is not God's nation, then pray tell me whose nation is it? It is either God's nation, or it is Satan's! Did Satan lead Columbus, a godly man, to our part of the world, or the Christian Pilgrims to this land to establish religious freedom, churches, Christian schools, raise up pastors, evangelists, and send missionaries around the world? Did Satan give birth to America? Certainly not! There is no in between. It was either God or Satan, and Satan cannot be against himself. On the other hand, Satan has tried to destroy the efforts of God to establish this nation. Folks, read the true history of our nation.

I hasten to say, however, that when I say this is God's nation, I do not mean it in the same sense that Israel is God's chosen people. Even though Israel is God's chosen people, her history contains great rebellion, great wickedness, and great idolatry. Even when God allowed His people to go into captivity, they were and still are His chosen people.

Humanly speaking, just because our own children commit sin, can we say that they are no longer our children? Our children remain our children by birth regardless of behavior. *Yes, America has been and now is very corrupt, and abounds in wickedness, and is far from being the "Christian nation" of the past. But it does not change the fact that God gave birth to this nation. Regardless of behavior, God is the Father of this great nation and this will always be true.*

Listen carefully, God raised up America as a banner—a standard to demonstrate to the world His great power and grace through His Son and our Lord and Savior Jesus Christ. If you study the **true** history of America, you will know that God put this nation together to declare Christ to the rest of the world. Our Founding Fathers were godly men who recognized God as our Creator and Jesus as the Christ, for the most part.

Listen to this great statement and promise from God's Book, the Bible: "Blessed is the nation whose God is the Lord" (Psalm 33:12). That's our nation, friend. *God has so greatly blessed America above all nations because our nation honored God all these years. We have witnessed His hand upon our nation from the beginning in protecting our land from foreign invasions.* This truth needs to be impressed upon our hearts so that we will not forget what God has done for our nation. *This is who we are and what we stand for; and we can be assured that this is the reason why the heathen nations want to destroy America.*

Why do multitudes of immigrants come out of poverty-stricken, persecuted, and religious-dictator tyranny and flock to this nation every year? They come because they desire what we enjoy and take for granted—our God-given freedom to worship without persecution, to educate our children, to go and come as we please, and to work and provide a living for our families in this great free-enterprise, industrialized nation. This freedom made us the wealthiest nation on the face of this planet. Again, this is why we honor God, and have **"In God We Trust"** as our national motto, inscribed on our currency and coins, and have **"One Nation Under God"** in our Pledge of Allegiance. This is why we honor God in the songs of America like *God Bless America, America the Beautiful,* and *God of Our Fathers, Whose Almighty Hand.* The religions of the world and their worship of false gods and idols have no songs to sing. Who or what would inspire them to sing? Think about it, have you ever heard them sing songs like ours to their false gods? What a great and LOVING God we worship!

Oh my friend, only a living eternal God can inspire words and music to songs like those, and the words to the song "Amazing Grace:"

> "Amazing grace! how sweet the sound, that saved a wretch like me!
> I once was lost, but now am found, was blind, but now I see.
> T'was grace that taught my heart to fear, and grace my fears relieved;
> How precious did that grace appear the hour I first believed!
> Thro many dangers, toils and snares, I have already come;
> Tis grace hath bro't me safe thus far, and grace will lead me home.

When we've been there ten thousands years, bright shining as the sun,
we've no less days to sing God's praise than when we first begun."

Yes, Americans have everything to sing about, especially Christians, for it was God who gave to us this nation and our eternal salvation. Satan wants to destroy our nation because America is truly God's nation, and secondly because:

B. America Is a Missionary Nation

In order to illustrate and give some basis for this statement, let us travel back in time more than two thousand years ago when Israel was looking for their Messiah to come and save them from their enemies, and reign over them as King. God from heaven sent His only begotten Son, the Lord Jesus Christ, to earth as the first missionary from heaven to His people Israel with a message of repentance and faith in Him as their true Savior and Messiah. But the Bible says that His own people as a nation rejected Him in disbelief, and had Him crucified on a cross. After His resurrection from the dead, and just before He ascended back to heaven, Jesus gave all His believing followers, including His twelve disciples a final commandment: "Go ye therefore, and teach all nations, baptizing them in the name of the Father, and the Son, and of the holy Ghost: Teaching them to observe all things whatsoever I have commanded you: and lo, I am with you always, even unto the end of the world"(Matthew 28:19-20).

The early Christian disciples went everywhere preaching and teaching the message of Christ, and multitudes believed, but the nation as a whole stayed in unbelief. Because of Israel's unbelief, and their rejection and ignorance of Jesus Christ, God has set them aside temporarily, and turned to all those who will believe, both Jews, and non-Jews (Gentiles), to be His witness throughout the world in this dispensation of grace.

John 1:12 says, "He came into his own, and his own received him not, but as many as received him to them gave he the power to become sons of God." From that time to the present, God has been building His Church (all true believers everywhere) to be a witness of the glorious Gospel of good news to a lost and dying world.

I personally believe that God has raised up America in these last days to be the center of missions for the evangelization of the world. Billy Graham said, "I believe America is truly the last bulwark of Christian civilization....We were created for a spiritual mission among nations."[9] As James Hefley, in *One Nation Under God*, said, "Even secular literature sounded the theme, as novelist Herman Melville unabashedly said: 'We Americans are the peculiar, chosen people—the Israel of our time; we bear the ark of the liberties of the world.'"[10]

Regardless of Israel's disobedience, our God is not left without a witness, and I believe that a great part of this witness for the past nearly four hundred years was America. No other nation on the face of this earth is like America. America's missionary vision is found in this great gospel hymn: "We've a Story to Tell to the Nations," sung in the churches across this great land of ours. Listen to some of the words of this inspired song:

> "We've a story to tell to the nations that shall turn their hearts to the right,
> a story of truth and mercy, a story of peace and light, a story of peace and light.
> For the darkness shall turn to dawning, and the dawning to noonday bright,
> and Christ's great kingdom shall come to earth, the kingdom of love and light."

What glorious and exciting words of love and truth! America has sent out more missionaries in the past preaching the gospel around the world than any other nation in the world. There are more churches in America than any other nation in the world. The story is told of a French historian who came to these shores early in American history to discover the secret of America's greatness. He returned to his country and penned these words: "I sought for the greatness and genius of America in her commodious harbors and her ample rivers, and it was not there; in her fertile fields and boundless prairies, and it was not there; in her rich mines and her vast world of commerce, and it was not there. Not until I went to the churches of America and heard her pulpits aflame with righteousness did I understand the secret of her genius and power. **America is great because she is good, and if America ever ceases to be good, America will cease to be great.**"[11]

Yes, there are more Bibles, and more Gospel proclaimed in and from America than any other nation in the world; and yet, **we are losing America! Satan in these last days is using all his power in workers of iniquity to deceive the non-Christians as well as multitudes of Christians.** I see our nation in a great spiritual battle for its very existence; our nation once honored God, but now we have turned our backs on God.

I encourage you to study the true history of America—Christian history, an incredible historical account, and discover why America stands alone above all nations over the face of this earth. You will find our Christian heritage a remarkable adventure in reading. Read it and reread it, and pass it on to your relatives, neighbors, and friends. And parents, if your children do not know what I am talking about, or even you parents, then I feel sorry for you. This is part of losing the spiritual battle that I am trying to unveil before your eyes—spiritual eyes that we allowed Satan to blind and deceive all these years. Satan wants to destroy our nation because we are a missionary nation. To be sure, we are in a gigantic spiritual battle—a battle to preserve America's Christian heritage, and prevent America's destruction.

Thirdly, Satan wants to destroy America because of

C. America's Moral Laws

This section is what I call the key to this book. It is the heart of the battle for America. This is the action section that determines your re-action to the rest of the book. Therefore, it is critical, dear friend, to read with an understanding heart, for it will determine your eternal destiny.

In the early years of America, moral laws practiced in our society were based on the Bible, the Word of God. We honored God in our homes, in the public schools, in business, and in government. Our young people became godly adult leaders of our nation in the schools, the colleges, and the government. Our nation was strong in the faith, and God blessed our nation in many ways, even with prosperity. For several generations, godly mothers and fathers taught their children the things of God and the commandments of God. Deuteronomy 6:5-7 says, "And thou shalt love the Lord thy God with all thine heart, and with all thy soul, and with all thy might. And these words, which I command thee this day, shall be in thine heart; And thou shalt teach them diligently unto thy children, and shalt talk of them when thou sittest in thine house, and when thou walkest by the way, and when thou liest down, and when thou risest up." These words of God were practiced in the early years of America.

But for the past generations, our families gradually backed away from teaching *the Word of God, which gives life, meaning, and direction to a person,* and we gave the teaching responsibility to the government-subsidized public school system. As time passed, we have tragically allowed all books and references to America's true Christian heritage to slowly disappear from our public schools along with the Bible, the moral laws, and prayer, without realizing what was taking place. Satan's work of deception slowly replaced God's Word in our schools and government with anti-God immoral practices. This continued through the years with little opposition or fanfare because our families departed from God and His Word. And because of this tragedy, multitudes of families to this day are still in the dark concerning the moral commandments of God!

Furthermore, our present generation has allowed the name of God and Jesus Christ, and anything with reference to the Christian faith **to be eliminated** from our public schools, colleges, and universities. And yet, we have allowed the religions of atheism, evolution, humanism, Eastern religious cultures, including the teaching of Islam in some states, to creep into our schools and universities. Dear friend, when a nation eliminates the moral laws of God, and proclaims Biblical morality to be irrelevant for today's society, as we are doing, that nation turns to anarchy, and total chaos is experienced where no right or wrong standards prevail. *Our nation is experiencing a moral and spiritual decay, the likes of which has never before been experienced in America.* Truly, these moral laws of God are as relevant for today's society as they were in the days of the Bible. We commit the same sins today as were committed in the Bible days. But today's generation has no knowledge of God and of His Word, or of His commandments.

Let us visit God's moral laws, found in Exodus 20:1-17, the ones most of us of the older generation may have heard before, but now have been rejected by multitudes of our younger generation.

Reasons Why Satan Wants to Destroy America

1. "Thou shalt have no other gods before me.
2. Thou shalt not make unto thee any graven image, or any likeness of any thing that is in heaven above, or that is in the earth beneath, or that is in the water under the earth. **Thou shalt not bow down thyself to them, nor serve them;** for I the Lord God am a jealous God, visiting the iniquity of the fathers upon the children unto the third and fourth generation of them that hate me. And shewing mercy unto thousands of them that love me, and keep my commandments.
3. **Thou shalt not take the name of the Lord thy God in vain;** for the Lord will not hold him guiltless that taketh his name in vain.
4. **Remember the sabbath day, to keep it holy.** Six days shalt thou labor, and do all thy work: But the seventh day is the sabbath of the Lord thy God: in it thou shalt not do any work, thou, nor thy son, nor thy daughter, nor thy maidservant, nor thy cattle, nor thy stranger that is within thy gates: For in six days the Lord made heaven and earth, the sea, and all that in them is, and rested the seventh day: wherefore the Lord blessed the sabbath day, and hallowed it.
5. **Honor thy father and thy mother:** that thy days may be long upon the land which the Lord thy God giveth thee.
6. **Thou shalt not kill** [the Hebrew word for kill is murder].
7. **Thou shalt not commit adultery.**
8. **Thou shalt not steal.**
9. **Thou shalt not bear false witness** against thy neighbor.
10. **Thou shalt not covet** thy neighbor's house, thou shalt not covet thy neighbor's wife, nor his manservant, nor his maidservant, nor his ox, nor his ass, nor any thing that is thy neighbor's."

These verses are often referred to as the "Ten Commandments" in their entirety; the bold words are the short version of the commandments. In these commandments, God reveals what our relationship should be toward Him, and toward one another. But more specifically, let us look at how these commandments should affect us as individuals: *In the first place*, the moral laws of God are like an x-ray mirror, showing us a spiritual look at what we are really like on the inside. Throughout these commandments, God says, "Thou shalt not," indicating that we are capable of breaking all of God's commandments, or His laws, and committing all the sins in His Book. This is just what the moral laws of God are designed to do—to show to all of His creation that we are sinners in the eyes of God. Romans 3:20 says, **"For by the law is the knowledge of sin."** Dear friend, this is how we know what is right and what is wrong—a moral standard for individuals, societies, and nations.

However, we should be cautious here and not try to do what multitudes of people are mistakenly trying to do—obey or to practice these laws thinking that God will be pleased and let them in heaven when they die. **But** God says, **"By the deeds of the law shall no flesh be justified"** (Romans 3:20). Again, I want to emphasize that *on our own* we may think we are doing a good job in keeping the law, but then we fail, or we break one of the *other laws*. You see friend, we may keep all of God's laws, but if we break just one of them, then we are guilty of breaking all of His laws—"For whosoever shall keep the whole law, and yet offend in one point, he is guilty of all. For he that said, Do not commit adultery, said also, Do not kill [murder]. Now if thou commit no adultery, and yet if thou kill, thou art become a transgressor of the law" (James 2:10,11). We are totally helpless in our sin nature and unbelief to change our condition. The reason is found in Romans 3:10-12, 23, "There is none righteous, no not one: There is none that understandeth, there is none that seeketh after God, there is none that doeth good, no, not one. All have sinned and come short of the glory of God."

So, now we can see how totally helpless we are to do anything that would please God, because of our sin nature. What we do, we do in our sin nature, and this is all that God sees! No matter how good we try to be, we find that we have *missed the mark—we have come short* of His moral standards, and that is why we are dying sinful creatures. That is an *absolute truth* that no one can deny. And the reason is given in God's Word, "**For the wages of sin is death...**" (Romans 6:23).

This must be awfully disappointing and shocking to multitudes of people who thought that by working at keeping the law, they would show to God that they deserve to go to heaven. Again, the laws of God are not only designed to show us that we are all sinners in the sight of God, but to show us how helpless we are in our sin. *Secondly*, the laws are designed to make us realize that we are in need of a Savior: "Wherefore the law was our schoolmaster to bring us unto Christ, that we might be justified by faith" (Galatians 3:24). Again, this is just what the moral laws of God are designed to do—to lead us to the only Savior for mankind, Jesus Christ.

You may be thinking, "If trying to keep the law will not profit me, then what can I do?" Listen carefully, and remember these words of God, which were given at the beginning of this section: "And thou shalt love the Lord thy God with all thine heart, and with all thy soul, and with all thy might" (Deuteronomy 6:5). God said these words several years *after* the Ten Commandments of Exodus. This is one of many commands of God, but a very important one because the *key word* in this commandment *is* **love**. *All the commandments of God* are wrapped up in that one commandment.

Let us quickly travel many hundreds of years later when Jesus, the Son of God, walked among His creation on this earth for a short time, and was asked the question, "What is the greatest commandment?" Jesus answered and said in Matthew 22:37-38,"*Thou shalt love the Lord thy God with all thine heart, and with all thy soul, and with all thy mind.*" This is the same commandment. In verse 38 Jesus said, "This is the first and great commandment." Then Jesus said in the next verses 39-40, "And the second is like unto it, *Thou shalt love thy neighbor as thyself*. On these two commandments hang all the law."

Many years later the Apostle Paul said the same thing about those two commandments in Romans 13:10, "Love is the fulfilling of the law." Friend, **this kind of LOVE WILL DO NO EVIL, OR HARM to our neighbor.** There would not be any hate, murder, rape, war, butchering of innocent people, and deceiving and lying to one another. *We would not have the mass murder of school children like we have heard about in many places in our nation, or other wickedness that is being practiced upon God's planet Earth!* Would we?

Friend, we cannot really love each other, let alone love God! *But Christ and His love for us can make all the difference.* Do you remember John 3:16? "For God so loved the world that he gave his only begotten son that whosoever believeth in him should not perish, but have everlasting life." God loves us, and Jesus His Son loves us so much that He died for us, and shed His blood for our sins. "Christ died for our sins" (1 Corinthians 15:31), "with the precious blood of Christ" (1 Peter 1:19). That is true love, unconditional love, the greatest love of all, and He wants us to return this kind of love. What a simple request! But, how can we do this? Well, this also is simple. Here is the answer to your question, "What can I do?" You must receive Christ into your heart. "As many as received him, [Jesus] to them gave he power [the authority, the right] to become sons of God, even to them that believe on his name" (John 1:12).

To receive Jesus means to realize, or believe that you are a sinner in the sight of God, and that Christ died for you to pay the penalty for your sin, and rose from the dead. Then, when this becomes a reality in your heart by faith, it becomes natural for you to repent, or to change your mind or heart about God and your sin. God says that He is "not willing that any should perish, but that all should come to repentance" (2 Peter 3:9). Now, in your mind *turn from your sin to Him with all your heart;* cry out to God to forgive you of your sin, and ask Jesus Christ into your heart to be your Savior and Lord of your life.

If you truly meant this with all of your heart, then Jesus saved you from all your sin. The Spirit of Christ comes to you to live within your heart, and gives you a new nature with power, *enabling you to have victory over your sin nature.* And, Christ will also *enable you to live for Him, and to love Him, and to love others, thereby keeping His commandments.* This is truly a **miracle; we will not have to struggle trying to keep the commandments of God,** and we will not want to do harm to anyone, but have a godly love in our heart for all people. This truly is the love of God. **A true Christian possesses in his heart a godly love for all people regardless of their behavior; and therefore, he would not have any desire to hurt or injure others. That is called unconditional love.** In a nutshell, it's God's love in our hearts that we return to God, thereby keeping these commandments. WOW!

Yes, God's great desire for *all of His creation* is to teach these moral truths to one another, and to our children. May God help us all to possess this kind of love! It is a gift from our God. Therefore, **God's laws are absolutely necessary in order for His creation to morally live together as individuals, as societies, and as nations; otherwise, there would be total chaos and destruction.** For these reasons the moral laws of our nation are being viciously attacked by all the forces of

Satan now more than ever before in our history, because of the impact they have on individuals, on our society, and on our nation. These are the reasons why Satan wants to destroy America: America is God's nation, America is a missionary nation, and America honors the moral laws of God.

A word of warning as I conclude this chapter: Just as Israel was so blessed of God, they became complacent and forgot God; they thought they had no need for God by thinking they had everything, and tragically departed from Him and were destroyed. I believe America is following in the steps of Israel. We are eliminating God's moral laws from our school system and society. We no longer have a need for the Ten Commandments in our public places and universities. One of the biggest reasons why we are where we are morally and spiritually is because we have become the richest nation in the world. In obtaining this great wealth, we have come to believe that we have everything and we no longer have a need for God in our nation. In other words, who needs God, for we have our own gods—wealth and prosperity! But God says in Deuteronomy 8:17-18, "And thou say in thine heart, My power and the might of mine hand hath gotten me this wealth. But thou shalt remember the Lord thy God; for it is he that giveth thee power to get wealth."

Make no mistake about it friend, without God we would not even be a nation, much less be the wealthiest nation in the world! What good is all the wealth in the world if our nation's morals are going down the tubes? The love of wealth and our trust in our wealth as our god are leading us down the road to moral and spiritual disaster. *Take heed, America, because our moral and spiritual condition is in an all-time critical stage, I mean critical and beyond critical! In other words, friend, we as a nation are on the brink of destruction and I do mean that!* You say, "I do not believe you," and I say to you and all Americans, "**Wake up** and look around! **Wake up** from your sleep and look where we are morally and spiritually!" And, I hasten to say that one does not have to look very far to realize our nation is *dying a tragic death.*

Jesus said in the Gospels, "We have eyes to see, but we see not, we have ears to hear, but we hear not." Most Americans are willingly blind and deaf to what is taking place. May I say this, dear friend, "Today most Americans (this includes a great number of those who profess to be Christians) do not know and do not care about what is going on in the real world. They do not have a clue as to what is taking place, and I must confess I was one of them for a long time. But most Americans live in a small world of their own. We work, eat, sleep, play; eat, sleep, work, play and the cycle goes on and on. Our attitude becomes indifferent, and we get to a place of who cares—'I have to think about my own family responsibilities. I do not have time to think about the state of this nation; I do not have time to get involved, and besides, this nation will take care of itself; it has in the past and it will now.'"

But God says in Ezekiel 22:30, "And I sought for a man among them, that should make up the hedge, and stand in the gap before me for the land, that I should not destroy it: but I found none." As you know, this was a disaster for Israel. God could not find anyone to make up a hedge, stand in the gap, and run with the footmen and horses. "Therefore have I poured out mine indignation upon them; I have consumed them with the fire of my wrath: their own way have I recompensed upon their heads, saith the Lord God" (Ezekiel 22:31).

God, however, has always had His voices standing in the gap, warning His people of on-coming judgment. God used Jeremiah, Ezekiel, and other prophets in the past to warn His people to take heed and take a stand. Today, God has raised up voices to warn the people of America. But, their voices are not being heard in a way that impacts our nation. I remember one such voice several years ago (I am sure there were others you can name). Over thirty-two years ago when communism was spreading around the world during the Vietnam era, God raised up a voice—John Stormer, a Baptist minister in Florissant, Missouri. He wrote a book called *The Death of a Nation*. It was read by multitudes of people, even the liberals, but received strong criticism from them. That is the way it goes when someone dares to speak out; there is going to be opposition from Satan.

After I read Stormer's book, God led me to distribute hundreds of copies of his book. Since then, God has given me a burden for America. Maybe some of you have read or recall this book and author. How about *None Dare Call It Treason*? The book is by the same author, John Stormer. I suggest that you read these books, if they are still in print. In my opinion, these books are still up-to-date. I mentioned John Stormer, and I will again later on in this book.

Our nation was in very bad shape then when communism was spreading like wildfire, but how much more now! We are beyond that period in time, and by the grace of God He spared our nation from destruction by lifting up another voice in President Reagan to put an end to communism, or did he? Yes, then, but now no, for communism is very much alive today in our nation. President Reagan was a strong fighter against communism before and after his election. God has spared our nation all these years. Will He spare our nation again? Read on, friend, open your eyes to the truth!

Today, along with John Stormer, there are others that are making up the hedge and standing in the gap, like former Supreme Court Judge Roy Moore of Alabama. Roy Moore is defending God's Word and standing in the gap for God and America. Roy Moore is fighting a raging battle with all the forces of Satan as he defends the Ten Commandments. I see him as a second Moses lifting high God's Ten Commandments, honoring God and America against a sea of satanic opposition. Roy Moore is one of the few who has dared to answer the call of God in Ezekiel 22:30. He is making up the hedge of righteousness, standing in the gap, and contending with the horses of Satan.

But multitudes of Americans never hear about those who are taking a stand for God and Country, because most of the time the secular news media rarely broadcast Christian news. The exception to this is when Christians are being attacked in public for speaking truth. And this is tragic. **What is more tragic** is that multitudes of professing Christians seldom listen to Christian radio and news; they seldom hear from pulpits about our sinful condition, but instead, hear nice sermons that tickle their ears, sending them home with a good feeling, while remaining **in the dark concerning our nation's condition. What a tragedy!** And this situation continues at home—they are busy surfing the internet, watching TV and soap operas that promote adultery, fornication, pornography, and filthy language without blinking an eye, as if God's moral laws did not exist. And Satan continues to keep the Church in darkness—**tragedy upon tragedy!**

Beloved, it is time to **wake up** *and open our spiritual eyes and ears and see the satanic forces raging their evil offensive battle within America before it is too late!* America has a moral problem far worse than anyone can imagine. I believe our moral condition is worse than Sodom and Gomorrah, worse than Hitler's atrocities, and I will describe next how I know that our nation's condition is beyond the critical point. You say, "That is preposterous!" But I say to you friend, "Your response is one of the reasons for the statement I just made, and for this book."

CHAPTER TWO

The Means by Which Satan Is Destroying America

IN THIS CHAPTER, I want to share with you the means by which Satan is bringing America down to a level of depravity, the likes of which have never been experienced before in our nation. I have identified what I believe to be *some* of today's satanic footmen and horses within and without America.

A. The Footmen in Our Midst

> *Jeremiah 12:5 "If thou hast run with the footmen, and they have wearied thee, then how canst thou contend with the horses? And if in the land of peace, wherein thou trustedst, they wearied thee, then how wilt thou do in the swelling of Jordan?"*

Before we can begin to identify the horses, we must first deal with the footmen. But first, let me define the word *run* from the previous verse. God speaks of running with the footmen. The word *run* normally means to run a race, run to get where you are going in a hurry, or to run after someone. However, in this verse it is not a physical race as such, but a spiritual race, meaning: to take a stand and speak out against evil, to oppose or resist evil, to warn people of danger ahead, to get involved, and to take action in defending the faith.

The Apostle Paul relates his spiritual life to a physical race when he says in 1 Corinthians 9:24, "Know ye not that they which run in a race run all." The Apostle Paul knew how to run with the Gospel of Christ against the forces of opposition. He gave his entire being to spreading the Gospel of Christ. He gave it his all. Now what are we to take action about, or against? Let us get really close to "home" with this first monster footman:

1. The Flesh (Self)

When I say *flesh*, I don't mean the skin covering our bones, but Biblically speaking, our whole being (self—soul, spirit and body) dominated by our sinful human nature referred to as "the natural man" in 1 Corinthians 2:14. Our flesh is therefore opposed to God. We cannot see our sin nature and likewise, we cannot see our soul and spirit, but we can experience the effects of our sin nature by our behavior. We are born with a sin nature, as we will see later on; and as such, we all have this footman in our lives. We cannot escape the flesh for it will be with us until we die; or as Christians, if what we call the "Rapture," meaning "catching away" takes place first, our body will be changed to a glorified sinless body like Christ (1 Thessalonians 4:16-17). But, while we are in this "body of death," as the Apostle Paul calls it in Romans 7:24, we must deal with it. Why do you say, "Deal with it?" *I mean that self, our flesh, is our number one enemy.*

Self is what stops many professing Christians dead in their tracks. It will oppose the Christian all the time when it comes to doing right because self wants control of us all the time. *For the non-Christian, self is in control—"self-centered,"* and as such, the person is totally helpless in his sin. He is as a dead person, or as the Apostle Paul says in Ephesians 2:1, "Dead in trespasses and sins." The unsaved person is dead to the spiritual things of God. Of course, this does not mean that an unsaved person is unable to do acts of human good or kindness, for it would be impossible for the human race to exist or live together if this were not true. However, I hasten to say that when the non-Christian uses his or her so-called goodness to gain favor with God, or uses their own goodness and kindness as the basis for entering heaven, God calls this kind of righteousness "filthy rags" (Isaiah 64:6). *Again*, in Romans 3:10,12, God says, "There is none righteous, no, not one; …there is none that doeth good, no, not one." As I have said earlier, anything we would do to try to offer up to God in exchange for heaven is totally unacceptable with God. No person can enter heaven with a sin nature and so-called good works—it is impossible, dear friend.

It is interesting to note that the Apostle Paul calls the Christian's sin nature "our old man" (Romans 6:6). The reason is because self should no longer be in power or control. However, there is a spiritual warfare going on within the Christian when that person starts to "run" for God, or to serve God as Paul says in Romans 7:23, "My members warring against the law of my mind.…"

But thanks be unto God, as Christians, we have the Holy Spirit within us to help us to have victory over the footman of flesh. Jesus said in John 15:5, "Without me ye can do nothing." Jesus also said in Luke 1:37, "For with God nothing shall be impossible." If we *allow* the "old man" to take control of our lives, it will be impossible for us to do anything for God and America. We will be useless and helpless to stand and *oppose the footman (our flesh)*. Consequently, Satan gets the victory. Later on in this chapter, I will again discuss how surprisingly our greatest enemy, the flesh, affects individuals and a nation.

At this time, I want to illustrate to you how helpless many professing Christians are when it comes to church attendance, Bible study, and prayer. For example, the Holy Spirit may whisper to you saying, "You need to go to church and spend time in prayer and studying the Bible." And self, your footman will agree sometimes and say, "Yes, you should go to the Sunday morning service since you have not been for a while. You should go every once in a while so you will be seen, and that certainly will please your fellow church members and your pastor. By the way, you do remember his name! But wait a minute, you know you cannot go to church Sunday night because you have a football game to watch, or a favorite TV program to watch, or is it a golf game you are going to play Sunday afternoon till late in the evening! Of course, this means you will be too tired and hungry to go to church Sunday night. And of course, Wednesday night service is totally out of the question because that is bowling night, or ladies' card game night, or you need to see that movie you have been wanting to see for a long time, or your 'worldly' neighbors are coming to visit. There is no way you can go this time! It is too inconvenient! And oh, there is certainly no time to read and study your Bible!"

Sound familiar? Many professing Christians never pray or read the Bible, let alone study it on their own apart from carrying it to church, or in many cases never carry a Bible to church. Friend, dear friend, *Satan works through our sin nature to get the victory*. The devil loves to bat us around like a rubber ball if we let him. It does not take much of an effort on the devil's part when he has control of self; we remain helpless in our flesh. Revival services during the week! Impossible, that is asking too much, Pastor! We have our week's agenda all lined up. And on and on it goes for the professing, backsliding Christians or unsaved church members.

For some time, a great number of churches have eliminated Sunday night and Wednesday night services, or turned them into social gatherings. Therefore, because of the times of the services, the vast majority of unsaved Americans never see Christians going to and from church, except to wake up in time to see them leaving the Sunday morning service. No wonder our nation is a spiritual disaster! Some Christians go on vacation and take a vacation from God. Beloved, we should be in the house of God during our vacation. I ask, "Where are all the Christians who should be speaking out against the horses that are destroying moral America?" Sadly, the answer rings out, "How can they speak out when they cannot get the victory over the footman of their flesh?" Satan has taken complete control, and they have been that way so long that they do not realize what has happened. The unsaved Americans see so-called "Christians" *doing* the same things as they do. Friend, I will tell you their condition—they are living for the flesh and therefore becoming stumbling blocks for the unsaved.

Also, I hasten to say, "a great number of 'professing Christians' who attend one or more services of the church rarely ever pray, read, or study their Bibles on their own, and never witness or speak out against the forces of evil." Listen carefully, *it is not enough to go to all the church services of the week, we must also spend some time each day praying to our heavenly Father, and studying His Word in order to have victory over self. Dear friend, if we cannot run with our flesh and get the victory, how on earth can we run with the horses, which are already upon us in our midst?* **Let us wake up from the dead,** open our spiritual eyes, and take a stand against the flesh and the devil before it is too late! The hour for America is late, very late!

God says in Hebrews 10:25, "*Not forsaking the assembling of yourselves together, as the manner of some is; but exhorting one another: and so much the more, as you see the day approaching.*" Listen to what God says in 2 Timothy 2:15, "Study to shew thyself approved unto God, a workman that needeth not to be ashamed, rightly dividing the word of truth." And the Psalmist says in Psalm 109:4, "I give myself to prayer." Again, God says in 1 Thessalonians 5:17, "Pray without ceasing."

America is in a shameful condition, beloved, and God help us when we stand before Christ ashamed! I cannot conceive of a person who claims to be a Christian never praying and reading the Bible! Can you? Is there enough evidence to convict you for being a Christian? The flesh gets the victory most of the time.

This leads us to the second footman in our lives called entertainment.

2. Entertainment

There is no doubt about it that this is a world of entertainment. Americans love to be entertained. And, *entertainment has become a god to many of us*—I mean we worship this god. Multitudes of Americans have been deceived into thinking we always have to be entertained. We think that we have to provide entertainment for our children so they stay happy and out of our hair.

Entertainment comes to us in many ways, but I want to zero in on a couple of major ones:

a. TV and movie industry

Electronics is a great invention; the TV is probably the greatest means of entertainment that has ever been invented.

The Means by Which Satan Is Destroying America

Most of this world now has TV. We can go everywhere, even across the ocean, and see everything we want without leaving our chair in our living room. Amazing! We sit for hour after hour as a family being *entertained and often being indoctrinated* by everything that is wicked and shameful on the TV. There are many who use the TV as a babysitter for their children. We can be entertained with just about anything we watch, including movies, sports, world news, religious programs, and even *"religious entertainment."*

Religious entertainment has crept into "Christian" radio, the Church, and is displayed on TV. One major religious network on TV is doing a *booming business* of bringing the world's "rock and rap" with all the loud noise, beat, dress, glittering lights, and mannerisms of the world into the Church, and into your living room calling it "Christian," or "Christian Rock." They are giving the Christian church a new look and sound called "contemporary music." I want to make it clear that I am not speaking about the older, or even some of the newer contemporary music, but let us call this latest by the right title in most cases, *contemptible satanic noise and sounds.* Dear friend, it really is unbelievable and tragic how Satan can deceive Christians. *Satan whispers* in our "bad" ear these words of inspiration: "We need to do something to reach our young generation; the *inspired* gospel hymns and songs are outdated. What we need to do is to dress up the worldly music by just adding Christian words. You see, you need to get the young people as well as the adults jumping and hollering and feeling good, and calling Jesus Christ 'JC' so you can win them over!"

Dear friend, do you know Satan is right? You will win them over to the "Jesus of Entertainment," but *not* the Jesus of the Bible. Jesus of the Bible is holy, righteous, and a consuming God *who hates the blaspheming of His Name.* Furthermore, Satan uses some of the voices of Christian singers in a worldly sensuous way so as to bring Jesus down to the level of sensuous love. And, it is this kind of singing and music that is creeping into Bible-believing churches, which is disgusting and blasphemous! Christian radio, on the one hand, plays good Christian Bible programs; but on the other hand, plays ungodly rock noise just because it carries a Christian label. Many of the unsaved entertainers are getting rich off of Christians—turning the Church into an "Entertainment Center" instead of a gospel-preaching "Evangelism Center."

God says in His Word, "Be not conformed to this world" (Romans 12:2). Let us not allow ourselves to embrace, or to fit into the mold of Satan's world system, including his "music." God says, "Wherefore come out from among them, and be ye separate saith the Lord" (2 Corinthians 6:17). May God help us to *see* this great deception of Satan, and *cast* it out of the Church, TV, and Christian radio!

We live in a world of entertainment, and yes, just about anything one can imagine is on TV and in the movies, including immorality, cursing, witchcraft, rebellion, murder, lying, stealing, cheating, and breaking all the Ten Commandments. **This is entertainment?** This is the kind of entertainment that destroys the soul.

Again, may we remember the ways Satan uses TV and movies: 1. To destroy our spirituality, our morals, our families, and our nation. No wonder family members are committing murder, rape, fornication, adultery, splitting up, and children are left alone without father or mother. 2. To keep our mind occupied, crippled and unaware of his on-going destruction of the home and America. We see this on display on the TV and the movies, yet to most of us watching TV day after day, it is a normal way of life. May God take the blinders from our eyes! Dear Christian parents, we allow ourselves and our children to bow before the TV and movie god, instead of bowing before our God in worship in the home. May God help us to come back to Him and experience His blessings on our families and on our nation! Dear God, open our eyes to what is going on in our American families.

b. Sports

The sports scene is another of America's favorite means of entertainment. Billions of dollars are being taken in, and some of the players are the highest paid people in America. For a great number of players, the love of money and drugs are destroying them. Imagine getting paid several million dollars a year for hitting a ball, running with a ball, chasing the ball, or throwing a ball in a basket! Unbelievable! We make them rich and we remain poor in comparison. I believe we have our values twisted. *Would to God, we would spend that time running the race for God!*

However, I do not mean to take anything from Christians who make a living in sports. If they feel God has placed them there to be a testimony to His glory, and to be faithful to God's Word, then I thank the Lord for them. But tragically, many viewers of sports, whether on TV or in the ballpark, allow it to become a god to them. We use the word *addicted* these days instead of *the worship of idols or gods* because it sounds better. We can allow sports to keep us out of the local community church, especially on Sunday, and from praying and reading our Bibles daily. And yes, we will be faithful to the TV and the sports players, but how faithful are we in giving of ourselves, and of our time to the Lord's work? Something for the Christian sports players to think about, as multitudes of people watch them play on Sunday instead of being in church!

I suppose I could go on and on, but I will let you take these two examples I have given and apply them to other entertaining things you do religiously. If we allow anything or anyone to take the place of God, then that is our god, and Satan's footman. You ask, "Do you ever watch TV or watch sports?" Yes, I do. I mainly watch the news now to keep up with what is going on around the world, and if I have the time, one favorite professional football team and one college football team.

I must ask a question at this point, since you ask me about watching TV and sports: Why would a Christian watch a TV program or movie where they use the word *"hell"* over and over? My guess is by now, we are not even aware that they do, because we have heard *"hell"* so often that it has become a household word. I took the time to check on this: It seems that 99 percent of programs and movies, with the exception of some of the real old family type movies, mention *"hell."* Also, many programs and movies either simulate engaging in immoral sex, or use words relating to immoral sex. Think about it parents! Think how this will affect your children, who sit there with you as they hear *hell* over and over, and watch immoral sex on display over and over! Parents, do you know that those who use *"hell"* that way are more than likely going to hell? Paid or not paid, hell is where they are heading if they do not get saved. Also, when we watch and expose our children to these kinds of programs and movies, we are supporting the work of Satan. *Dear Christian parents, does that bother you?*

I work among all kinds of people every day and I hear them say, "Oh, hell" as normal conversation. Parents, the TV medium is promoting this kind of stuff across America and we Christians are encouraging Satan to continue to take away the fear of hell! On the other hand, we go to church and hardly ever hear the preacher mention *"hell"* the proper way, or speak out on the sins of society! Why? Because we do not want to offend anyone! We want to keep our people coming to church. We do not want to lose our members. May God help us, and open our eyes so that pastors will preach the whole council of God.

Does that answer your question why I do not have any desire to watch those promoters of wickedness? *If all who profess to be Christians stop watching this kind of programming, the TV industry and the Hollywood crowd would soon change what they say and show.*

Satan's desire is to entertain American people to death. In the book of Revelation chapter 2 and 3, we find the Lord Jesus describing the spiritual condition of several churches in the time of the Apostle John's day. He described one church as being "luke-warm, and neither cold or hot, I will spue you out of my mouth" (Revelation 3:16). The word *"lukewarm"* describes what is, and has been spreading like wildfire throughout the churches today. I mean this is of epidemic proportion! Most churches have all but self-destructed because they are not able to overcome or run with the flesh, and the entertainment footman. Again, Satan uses these tools to render the Church lukewarm, and to keep our minds off the major horses that are destroying America. My *friend, if you cannot run with these footmen, what are you going to do about the horses which are now upon us in our midst like a flood (the swelling of Jordan)?* "Let us lay aside every weight, and the sin which doth so easily beset us, and let us run with patience the race that is set before us" (Hebrews 12:1).

The flesh is the Christian's number one enemy, and the world of entertainment greatly diminishes our chances of getting victory over our flesh, thus eliminating us from the race set before us. My friend, what footmen do you have in your life that are keeping you from victory, and from taking a stand for the cause of Christ and for America? Think about what I have just asked! We are truly in a race for our nation's survival, but tragically we are asleep to a relentless takeover of America by the forces of Satan. Read on friend!

B. The Horses in Our Midst

I want to begin with a couple of statements that most Americans will not believe, or will not accept: *America is under siege by Satan's footmen and horses. Satan has established a secure beachhead, and is well on his way to completely taking control of our nation while most Americans are asleep and willingly ignorant of our desperate situation.* Some of us are "seemingly" aware of this situation, yet we are so caught up in the things (footmen) of this world that we do not have time to be concerned about the creeping evil monsters that are slowly devouring our nation. As a result, our nation is finding it impossible to run with these horses and overcome them; thus, the spiritual battle for truth is being lost. If you have not guessed by now the identity of these horses, then I shall state another truth, which should identify a couple of them: *Dear friend, the moral condition of our nation is beyond Sodom and Gomorrah, and beyond Hitler's atrocities! Our nation is beyond the critical stage!*

Let us look at some of these horses within our nation:

1. Homosexuals and Lesbians

I shall preface my discussion with what may be an alarming statement to a great number of the reading audience because it will be hard to receive, especially since a great number have already made up their minds on this matter. However, I challenge you to have an open mind as you read through this section. We as a society and nation have allowed and let loose a gigantic destructive horse in these homosexuals and lesbians. History has proven morally and physically that this choice to sin brought about the leveling of cities to ashes—like ancient Sodom and Gomorrah in the land of Palestine. Again, *I challenge the reader to stay with me and read through the entire book. This is so important.*

A great number of Americans have indoctrinated themselves, as well as others, into believing that homosexuality is hereditary—it is genetic; just another healthy lifestyle, and natural healthy acts of love. The popular term is "sexual orientation" or "sexual preference." However, *based on the authority of the Word of God, homosexuality is a sin of the worst kind of behavior.* In fact, God calls it an abomination!

Listen to what God says about homosexuals in Leviticus 18:22, "Thou shalt not lie with mankind as with womankind: it is abomination." Does that sound like homosexuality is hereditary, in the genes, or sexual orientation? No, it is not inherited, but rather a *behavior problem. All sin is a behavior problem, from lying, stealing, raping, adultery, fornication, and disobedience to murder.* If the homosexual lifestyle and all the other sins were inherited, God would not have given this commandment as well as the others. What was inherited from Adam, however, was our sin nature. *Nowhere* in the Word of God do we find God giving this commandment, "Thou shalt not have a sin nature, it is abomination." Our sin nature is part of our being, our makeup, our genes from our mother's womb, as stated in Psalm 58:3, "The wicked are estranged from the womb: they go astray as soon as they be born, speaking lies."

Therefore, we are helpless to undo what we have inherited from Adam, the first creative being. Due to our sin nature, we are capable of misbehaving and committing every sin that is mentioned in the Book, including that of the homosexuals and lesbians. However, **we have the ability to choose** to sin or not to sin. Think about that friend! Almost everything we do in life involves making a choice. God says, "Choose you this day whom ye will serve" (Joshua 24:15); "I have set before you life and death…therefore choose life" (Deuteronomy 30:19). Dear friend, to choose to follow and serve God is eternal life! To choose to follow and serve Satan is eternal death! This is very important. God has enabled us to make that choice. Therefore, God holds us accountable for the decisions we make in life concerning doing the right thing or doing the wrong thing. This is the reason why He can give a commandment like that of Leviticus 18:22, and the Ten Commandments. It is our choice to obey or not to obey. I am glad our loving God gives us the ability to make choices in life. Listen to this convincing Scripture:

> *1 Corinthians 6:9-10,11 "Know ye not that the unrighteous shall not inherit the kingdom of God? Be not deceived: neither fornicators, nor idolaters, nor adulterers, nor effeminate, nor abusers of themselves with mankind, [homosexuals] nor thieves, nor drunkards, nor revilers, nor extortioners, shall inherit the kingdom of God...such were some of you...."*

The Apostle Paul is reminding some that this was your lifestyle, but you no longer practice these sins.[1]

I trust that you are allowing your mind to *take in* the things that have been said thus far. But you say, "I do not accept the Bible." You are part of multitudes who believe the same thing, but does that make it right for you? A lot of people murder one another! Does that make it right for you to do the same? I think you would agree with me that because others murder, it does not give you the right to murder another person. Therefore, you have to come up with a superior standard that gives you the basis or justification for your actions! Friend, can you produce this "standard?" I think not. It is like saying, "I do not believe two plus two equals four." That does not change the fact that two plus two equals four. Dear friend, we have in our society the laws of physics, math, of nature, *and the laws of morality*, which are based on God's Word! Friend, we do not possess a better standard than our

Creator! Let us look at what happened in the beginning of the human race in order to reinforce what has been said.

Genesis 1:26-27 says, "And God said, Let us make man in our image, after our likeness…So God created man, in the image of God created he him; male and female created he them." In the beginning, God created man in His image and likeness. This means God created man and woman (Adam and Eve) as spirit beings, for God is a Spirit; as moral beings, for God is sinless; as communicative beings, for God is the Great Communicator; and as the shining-glory likeness of God, for God is totally engulfed in brightness and glory. In other words, God created man as a reflection of His image and likeness, clothed in a body formed out of the dust of the earth (Genesis 2:7). This was God's creation yet *untested*.

Then came God's test to His creation, His first command and warning: "Of every tree of the garden thou mayest freely eat; But of the tree of the knowledge of good and evil, thou shalt not eat of it; for in the day that thou eatest thereof thou shalt surely die" (Genesis 2:16-17).

This is the beginning of man's responsibility. God gave His creation a choice to obey, or not to obey, and man made the wrong choice. Man *disobeyed* God's Word, and as a result, lost the image and glory of God, was engulfed in a sin nature, and spiritually and physically became a dying race.

Romans 5:12 says, "Wherefore, as by one man sin entered the world, and death by sin; and so death passed upon all men, for that all have sinned."

Why did they make the wrong choice? The answer is in the Word of God. Satan came to Eve in the Garden of Eden in the form of a serpent and said to her in Genesis 3:1, "Hath God said, Ye shall not eat of every tree of the garden?" Eve answered and said in so many words, "Yes, lest ye die." Then Satan said to Eve, "Ye shall not surely die" (verse 4).

Satan kept on contradicting God's Word and telling Eve that the tree was something that would make her wise and be as gods. Eve bought into it, went after Adam and relayed the message to him, and they disobeyed God's commandment—*His Word.* They died immediately, spiritually separated from God, and eventually died physically. The process of death continues within the whole human race. We are a dying race because of disobedience *by making the wrong choice.* You see God's Word came true! We are living proof of it, or should I say, "Dead proof!"

The point I want to make is that Satan has not changed—he is still the master **deceiver**, deceiving multitudes of people every day by his same lies, and contradicting God's Word saying, "Homosexuality is not a sin, because we are born that way." Do you see friend where you are getting your thoughts? Satan is the father of deception and lies, and he passes it on, as Eve did to Adam. Adam and Eve believed the lies of Satan. They chose to disobey God's Word resulting in death instead of life. Disobedience is sin. Disobedience brings forth all kinds of sin. But it is a choice, not an hereditary trait.

God created a man and woman of opposite sex for a purpose. Men with men, and women with women *are not* genetically (naturally) attracted to each other. On the other hand, God genetically (naturally) attracts and equips men and women for each other for the purpose of biologically producing children. God said to Adam and Eve (man and woman), "Be fruitful and multiply" (Genesis 1:28).

God gave the commandment in Leviticus 18:22 because of His omniscience (all knowing); He knew that the sin nature of man *is capable of committing any sin by choice because of unbelief and disobedience.* Again, God says in Leviticus 20:13, "If a man also lie with mankind as he lieth with woman, both of them have committed an abomination: they shall surely be put to death; their blood shall be upon them." My friend, that is a really strong statement, but *it is from God our Creator.*

Listen again to what God said over a thousand years later in Romans 1:26-27, "For this cause God gave them up unto vile affections: for even their women did change the natural use into that which is against nature; and likewise also the men leaving the natural use of the woman, burned in their lust one toward another; men with men working that which is unseemly, and receiving in themselves that recompence of their error." And verse 32 says, "Who knowing the judgment of God, that they which comment such things are worthy of death, not only do the same, but have pleasure in them that do them."

Friend, *can you see* **choice** *throughout those verses?* It should be very clear to anyone who is seeking the truth. God calls this sinful behavior "vile affections, against nature." Beloved, *homosexual and lesbian behavior is "against nature" defiling a society and "worthy of death."* I did not say that, God said it. If we say that is not so, then we call God our Creator a liar! Hebrews 6:18 says it is "impossible for God to lie." Are we going to argue with our Creator? Who are we to think otherwise! Who are we to argue with the one who created us! If we go against God and say He is wrong, then we set ourselves up as gods, just like Adam and Eve did in the garden. How then can we as a society and nation close our eyes on this kind of behavior? Nowhere in the Bible does God condone sodomy.

You may be asking, "Should all homosexuals and lesbians be put to death?" Good question. Notice, if you will, the statement in Leviticus 20:13, "shall surely be put to death," and the statement in Romans 1:32, "worthy of death." God says in one place "shall surely be put to death," and in the another place, almost fifteen hundred years later, "worthy of death." The difference is Jesus Christ, the Son of

God. Between the two sayings, Jesus Christ came to us and willingly took on flesh like our flesh; took *all* our sins, including the sin of sodomy, and died on the cross with our sin, in *our place* to *pay our sin debt*. After His resurrection from the dead, Jesus Christ is now at the right hand of the Father waiting to forgive *all* of our sin, change our lives, and make us new creations in Christ Jesus. WOW, what a Savior!

My friend *we are all worthy of death*, but God has given his creation another chance—a *choice* to rectify our condition. If we choose to believe what Christ has done for us, repent of our sins, and receive Him as our personal Savior and Lord, then He forgives us and saves us from our sin. And we will live and reign with Christ for all eternity. Will you make the right decision this time? *Our loving God is and has given us time to repent of our sins and the sin of unbelief, for He "is longsuffering to us-ward, not willing that any should perish, but that all should come to repentance" (2 Peter 3:9).*

However, I *hasten* to remind again my dear homosexual and lesbian friends to listen to God *on this side of the cross* when He says that He "gave them up unto vile affections." There comes a time when God lifts His restraining, convicting grace from those who worship in their unnatural affections, and whose conscience does not bother them, to live out the wicked desires of their heart to their own destruction. Friends, this kind of behavior has been demonstrated toward God on display in our public streets, and protected by our police with our tax dollars. They laugh at authority, mock Jesus, and some parade around in the nude simulating their acts of wickedness as if their sin was not sin, and there were no God.

God says, "The show of their countenance doth witness against them; and they declare their sin as Sodom, they hide it not. Woe unto their soul! for they have rewarded evil unto themselves" (Isaiah 3:9). My friend, **this is a very dangerous and tragic heart condition, especially when our God-given** conscience no longer functions as an accuser. It could mean one's chances of being delivered from this sin is very slim. If you feel in your heart any conviction at all that what you are involved in is wrong, I beg of you to turn from your sin to God. Tell Him you are sorry, throw yourself on the mercy of God and ask Jesus Christ to come into your heart and save you from your sin now while the window of opportunity exists. And if you truly mean it, He will honor your desire and make you a different person.

Also, there is another law of God that never changes and that is the law of sowing and reaping. The Bible says in Galatians 6:7-8, "Be not deceived; God is not mocked: for whatsoever a man soweth, that shall he reap. For he that soweth to his flesh shall reap corruption; but he that soweth to the Spirit shall of the Spirit reap life everlasting." This is God's law of nature. *For the homosexuals and lesbians, it means AIDS, a slow, or quick death.* I believe many are dying, maybe ten, fifteen, twenty some years prematurely because of AIDS, killer drugs, and diseases associated with this kind of reckless and vile behavior. This is the tragedy of self-destruction. **If the homosexual lifestyle is as they say, "natural healthy acts of love," then why are they dying this way? Think about it!**

How scary, foolish, dangerous, and final these words would be for you to continue in your sin, die, and spend a conscious eternity in hell and the lake of fire in torment. You will be separated from your Creator and your God who loves you more than human words can describe. Yes, I would say that is a death of all deaths.

Dear friend, I know the things that God has said above are hard to accept, but God cares for us, His creation, so much that He has given us His instruction book, the Bible, to show us the way of eternal life—His life. We have been given a choice in this life to live one of two ways: "Enter ye in at the strait gate: for wide is the gate, and broad is the way, that leadeth to destruction, and many there be which go in thereat: Because strait is the gate, and narrow is the way, which leadeth unto life, and few there be that find it" (Matthew 7:13-14). We can *choose* the way of eternal death, or the way of eternal life. This is the kind of loving Creator we have in Christ Jesus. He has given us a choice.

I want to reemphasize *how much God loves us. I cannot emphasize this enough.* I remember watching the news on TV, and a certain homosexual was marching down the street holding up a sign that read, "Jesus loves homosexuals." I thought to myself, he is right! If I were there, I would have run to him, hugged him and said, "God does love homosexuals and lesbians and all people regardless of our **behavior**." John 3:16 says, "For God so loved the world, [that means all of us] that he gave his only begotten Son, [died for us] that whosoever [that means all of us] believeth in him, should not perish, [that means eternal separation from God] but have everlasting life." [everlasting life is eternal life].

This was no doubt the greatest demonstration of love known to man. God's love knows no boundaries, no limitations, no conditions, or restrictions; and therefore, His love is unconditional. But this love of God that is holy, righteous, and just, demands a penalty be paid for sin; and therefore, His justice must be satisfied. A penalty, a price for sin has to be paid if we choose to reject God's Word, stay in our sin, and die that way. This penalty is conscious eternal separation from God after physical death.

But the good news is that Jesus Christ satisfied the holiness of God's righteous demands by paying our sin debt for us, including separation from God, His own Father, so that we will not have to pay this terrible penalty ourselves. Jesus Christ, the God-man, rose from death, and is now sitting at the right hand of the Father, **victorious** over sin, death, and

Satan. Jesus is waiting to forgive and save all who will ask Him for forgiveness, believe on Him, and receive Him as Lord and Savior of their lives. He will change your lifestyle.

> *"If any man be in Christ, he is a new creature; old things are passed away; behold, all things are become new" (2 Corinthians 5:17).*

No longer is separation from God in this life experienced, nor after death! That is a promise from our loving God.

Dear reader, you may be asking me, "Why are you doing this, or writing all this?" My answer is found in the above paragraph. When God saves a person, and this is true of all real Christians, His Spirit takes up residence in that person's heart to live with the person forever. And with the Spirit comes the love of God. So, my answer is, *I love you with a godly love, and care about you as well as all people.* If I did not love you and care about you, I would not have written this book. I would not care what happens to you or America.

Allow me to illustrate what I am trying to say: Picture yourself driving your car down the road, and it is very foggy. Ahead of you is a person, whom you cannot see yet because of the fog. The person is waving a red flag as he begins to see the lights of your car. The person knows something you do not know—you are approaching a bridge that has collapsed. It will mean certain death for you if you continue on this road. As you proceed to drive, you see the person waving the red flag, but you *ignore the waving of the flag* and continue on to your death. What a tragedy! You had a choice, but you made the wrong choice, and it cost you your life. The person waving the flag is yours truly, as well as thousands of others. The flag represents the Bible, and the fog represents the blindness of the heart. "The god of this world hath blinded the minds of them which believe not" (2 Corinthians 4:4). Satan is "the god of this world."

I am as thousands out there who love and care for you. Would you call this hate? Notice also, that in a situation like this, the driver of the car notices the flag more than the person. A person standing *without a flag* would hardly be noticed as one continues to drive down the road. What would you think of a person who knew that certain death was just a short distance away and did not try to flag you down? Which would you call this, love or hate? The tragedy is that millions of people, saved as well as unsaved, realize the danger that lies ahead for homosexuals, lesbians, *and America*, but only a few will dare to raise the red flag. However, the true church is a friend of homosexuals and lesbians—an open door of caring, of love, of truth and help to all people regardless of behavior problems. That is something to think about and to remember as you read the rest of this book. Are you still with me? I trust that you are and that you will promise to continue to read the entire book, and ask God to speak to your heart. Thank you my friend, you have come this far, read on.

Let us look together at the cities of Sodom and Gomorrah, and what God had to say about the behavior of these people, and how He dealt with the situation.

In Genesis 13:10, we begin with the account of Abraham, who was called Abram at that time, and Lot, Abram's brother's son. Each of them owned large herds of cattle. Abram decided to separate himself from Lot in order to keep from having problems (verses 5-8). Lot chose the land as described in verse 10, a land that was "well watered everywhere…even as the garden of the Lord, like the land of Egypt." This garden was the "Garden of Eden" that had everything for man's needs. Maybe the cities of Sodom and Gomorrah were like the land of America—a land of water everywhere, and a land of plenty, a good land. I do not believe there is another land in this aspect like America in the world. We are blessed by God to be privileged to live in His great nation, America.

Verse 13 says, "But the men of Sodom were wicked and sinners before the Lord exceedingly." I strongly believe God is saying the same thing today to America—the men and women who practice sodomy are exceedingly wicked sinners. God has not changed His mind about sin—*Malachi 3:6 "I the Lord change not."* Sin is still sin. The Bible, God's Word remains the same, including issues of immorality, because people are still the same especially when it comes to morals. *We commit the same sins that were committed in the Bible days.* This is something that America needs to learn and heed, *or be destroyed.* God gives this warning in 2 Peter 2:6,

"And turning the cities of Sodom and Gomorrha into ashes condemned them with an overthrow, **making them an ensample unto those that after should live ungodly."**

Now let us read the rest of the story about the cities of Sodom and Gomorrah: Chapter 14 of Genesis tells us that a confederation of the kings of nations went against the kings of Sodom and Gomorrah, Bera and Bitsha, and apparently wounded them. The kings raided both cities, took everything of value, and took Lot captive. One man escaped and came to Abram and told him everything. Abram assembled an army and went after these kings; they smote them and rescued Lot, his goods, the women, the people, and returned to Sodom.

I briefly reviewed chapter 14 to say that the cities of Sodom and Gomorrah were large enough to have kings, and yet *very small* compared to most of our major cities. The entire region of Palestine, sometimes called the "Holy Land of Israel" from the river of Egypt to the river of Euphrates (Genesis 15:18), (depending on where you measure along the Euphrates in the north) could be about the size of the state of New Jersey. Others compare it to the state of Maryland. The entire land of Israel, as we can see, is very small in comparison to America. And when we think of *the cities of Sodom and Gomorrah, they have to be very small* in comparison to most of our major cities.

Think about this comparison as I continue my discussion, because I want to bring what I have just said back up later on in this book. Abram rescued Lot and brought him back to Sodom. A few years later, God said to Abram (now called Abraham) in Genesis 18:20–22, "And the Lord said, because the cry of Sodom and Gomorrah is so great, and because their sin is very grievous...." What sin is God speaking of when He said, "very grievous?" God sent two angels to Lot to bring him, his wife and two daughters out of the city before He destroyed it. God says in Genesis 19:4-5,

> "The men of the city, even the men of Sodom, compassed the house round, both old and young, all the people from every quarter: And they called unto Lot, and said unto him, Where are the men which came in to thee this night? Bring them out unto us, that we may know them."

And, Lot said in verse 7, "Do not so *wickedly*." My friend, the grievous and abominable sin was homosexuality. Notice the men of the city called out for the men in the house that were with Lot, *not his daughters, but the men* (in this case they were angels with Lot) so that they may "know them"—*have sexual relations with them.* It is interesting to note that these same words and actions of men were said many hundreds of years later in the book of Judges, chapter 19:22-24, "we may know them" and "do not so wickedly." Make no mistake about it friend, these are homosexuals.

Abraham became an intercessor for the people of Sodom, an outsider standing in the gap attempting to spare the cities. In Genesis 18:23-33, Abraham asked God, "Wilt thou also destroy the righteous with the wicked?" In the following verses Abraham tries to bargain with God, asking to spare the city for "the fifty righteous." Abraham actually thought there were fifty righteous people in Sodom. Abraham continued to bargain until it was down to ten righteous people, and God could not find even ten. *All that was left was Lot, his wife and two daughters. Out of all the people in these two cities, God could only find four people (Lot's family) who were not homosexuals, lesbians, or sympathizers.* Where were all the people who should have been alarmed at this wicked horse when there were only a few homosexuals? They should have made up a hedge by taking a stand for righteousness in the gap, and speaking out against this sin before they were engulfed in wickedness.

Dear friend, there are already a large number of homosexuals in our nation, and in high places of influence and rapidly taking charge, but still few in comparison to the total population of America. How many does it take to be in control? Read on my friend, and I trust you will get a sense of urgency in what I am trying to convey. Friend, there is no time to be idle! We need to rise up now, and take a stand, speak out and put down this evil before it brings America down! This is spiritual warfare!

The unsaved homosexuals and lesbians lack understanding because morality is spiritual.

> *"But the natural man receiveth not the things of the Spirit of God; for they are foolishness unto them; neither can he know them, because they are spiritually discerned"* (1 Corinthians 2:14).

The Bible speaks to our spirit, not to the flesh. Therefore, what they do not understand, and if it interrupts their way of having fun in their so-called lifestyle, they fight against and call it *"hate"* from those who disagree with them.

Again, only Lot and his two daughters were left and God spared them. Lot's family was commanded by God not to look back, but Lot's wife disobeyed and was turned into a **pillar of salt** because *she had sympathy for the wicked.* Abraham thought that out of all the thousands of people who may have populated these two cities, there would surely be at the least fifty righteous people. Would you think so? I certainly would have thought **that there would have been more than fifty. But, chapter 19 verse 4 says *all* were homosexuals, lesbians, and no doubt included in the "all" were homosexual sympathizers. Do you** suppose that if they had a *police force, mayor, governor, senators and congressmen* like we have today, they would have been included in the "all?"

I am sure that in the beginning stages of these two cities, when there were only a handful of homosexuals and lesbians, the leaders never dreamed this sin would take over these two cities and turn them *all* into homosexuals, lesbians, and sympathizers. *Beloved, talk about terrorist destruction, this is destruction of the worst kind—moral destruction resulting in physical destruction. Think about it! All the people including the city's high officials and their kings became involved in the homosexual cause.*

This same situation is happening in our nation *now,* including some of the leadership of this nation. Some of our big businesses are involved as well, either for personal and political reasons, or to stay in business. I believe that not only the homosexuals and lesbians are unrighteous, but also sympathizers. Those who do not speak out against their cause, and all those who for political reasons willingly support, or else are coerced into supporting their cause are partakers of their sins.

The Bible says, "And have no fellowship with the unfruitful works of darkness, but rather reprove them" (Ephesians 5:5-7,11). You say, "I am not sure I believe all that." Again,

God's Word says, "God is not a man, that he should lie" (Numbers 23:19), "Let God be true and every man a liar" (Romans 3:4), "God that cannot lie" (Titus 1:2), and it is "impossible for God to lie" (Hebrews 6:18).

Maybe what you are really trying to say is this, "I do not want to believe what you are saying; it is not my business, and I have to think about my family, job, and social interests. I am too busy to get involved." These are the people without a flag in their hand. If this is the mind of most Americans, and it looks like we are fast approaching this mind-set, then I say, "Move over Sodom and Gomorrah and make room for America!" May God help us, friend. Is this what we really want to see happen to our nation—this precious gift from God? Are we going to allow the ones who sacrificed so much and gave their lives in the beginning of our nation to the present time to die in vain by allowing Satan to destroy our nation?

Let us read *again* what our loving God says about this abominable sin in Romans 1:26-27,

> *"For this cause, God gave them up unto vile affections: for even their women did change the natural use into that which is against nature. And likewise also the men leaving the natural use of the woman, burned in their lust one toward another, men with men working that which is unseemly, and receiving in themselves that recompense of their error."*

And verse 32, "Who knowing the judgment of God, that they which commit such things are worthy of death, not only do the same, but have pleasure in them that do them."

If their lifestyle were as they say, "*natural healthy acts of love,*" *why then would God say these things about this lifestyle, and destroy Sodom and Gomorrah?* **Think about that!** People never change; Satan just dresses up sin, and calls it "just another healthy lifestyle preference, or sexual preference that should not face discrimination." If we do speak out in opposition, it becomes a "hate crime." Dear friend, this sin is gross, disgusting, and degrading, sinking to the lowest level of human depravity. This is incredible blindness. Again, God says, "The god of this world hath blinded the minds of them which believe not" (2 Corinthians 4:4).

Let us look at what is happening today to the homosexual movement and what they are accomplishing. Remember, my subject is "The Battle for America, A Game of Life or Death, The Footmen and Horses in Our Midst." This is a spiritual battle that is being fought—evil versus the good, righteousness versus unrighteousness, and God versus Satan. Make no mistake about it friend, this is what it is all about. The homosexuals have a very carefully thought-out, planned agenda to take control of America. They are actively using whatever means possible to obtain their demands as set forth in their agenda, and distributed over ten years ago at the "Gay Pride" march on Washington, D.C., *April 25, 1993.*

Listen to their demands:

1. "Demand the repeal of all sodomy laws and legalization of all forms of sexual expression (including pedophilia, changing age of consent laws to allow sex with youth).
2. Demand defense budget funds be diverted to cover AIDS patients' medical expenses, and taxpayers funding of sex change operations.
3. Demand the legalization of same-sex marriages, and legalization of adoption, custody, and foster care within these structures.
4. Demand the full inclusion of lesbians, homosexual men, bisexuals and transgenders in education and childcare.

5. Demand that contraceptives and abortion services be made available to all persons, regardless of age.
6. Demand taxpayer funding for artificial insemination of lesbians and bisexuals. Forbid religious-based concerns regarding homosexuality from being expressed (as is the case on radio and TV in Canada).
7. Demand that organizations, such as the Boy Scouts, be required to accept homosexual scoutmasters."[2]

Today, over ten years later, the homosexuals are vigorously in the process of enforcing all of these demands into laws and practice. *And what are we doing about it? We cannot be silent any longer! Again I say, get involved, join forces, rise up, make up a hedge, stand in the gap, take a stand, speak out against this evil. Let us run with these horses and God will give us the victory!* If we do not speak out and let our senators, congressmen, governors, and our president *know our concerns and demands*, then nothing will be done—and that is a vote for evil.

Remember when the Democrats held their National Convention in 2001? The Boys Scouts marched in *waving the American flag*, and they were *booed!* **This was unbelievable, but true.** Who would have thought this would be happening in America! This gives us some idea of the influence and spread of the homosexual movement across our land.

More recently, another "demand" called "hate crime" was added to their agenda. Again, what it is all about is simply this: If we disagree with their so-called lifestyle and agenda, and oppose them forcing their sick lifestyle upon our society, they cry out "hate." And we Americans are falling for this deception. *They again equate opposition with hate, bigotry, intolerance, and prejudice.*

The homosexual activists are pressuring our nation's top leaders, especially liberal Democrats into passing this bill nationwide, calling it a "Non Discrimination Bill." But the fact of the matter is that the homosexuals are the *haters*. They hate anyone who opposes them and their agenda, and they plan to destroy them. Why were the Boys Scouts booed? It was because of hate from the homosexual sympathizers in the crowd—the homosexuals lost their case for a leadership spot, because the Scouts refused to take in homosexuals. The Boys Scouts should have been *applauded* for their stand. Dear friends, the Boy Scouts are an example of making up a hedge, standing in the gap, and running with the horses with the truth to victory. May God give us more Americans who will take a stand for God and America! May God richly bless these Boy Scouts, and may they gain more support for their stand. This should be the daily prayer for all decent people.

My friend, if the Boy Scouts can take this kind of stand with such opposition, how much more should we be making up a hedge of righteousness, standing in the gap, and running with the truth of God's Word to victory! Warning, my friend: Again, *those who support evil are partakers of their evil deeds, and those who do not speak out against evil are with the evildoers!*

Jesus said, "He that is not with me is against me" (Matthew 12:30). On whose side are you? Friend, where do you stand? As a result of the homosexual's defeat, they are vigorously and forcefully going about to destroy the Scouts by pressuring businesses and organizations to cut off all their financial support for the Boy Scouts or boycott their businesses. *That is coercion, hate and also extortion!* They are trying to coerce schools into not allowing the Scouts to meet in their facilities. It has been working, folks. **If their lifestyle is as they say, "natural healthy acts of love," then why do they have to use force and terrorism on our society for acceptance?** Think about that, friend! It seems that multitudes are deceived and are bowing down to this wickedness instead of taking a stand.

The homosexuals failed to infiltrate the Boy Scouts, but they recently infiltrated the Big Brothers and Big Sisters of America organization nationwide. Parents, this is an organization that has been entrusted with the care of your children! I strongly suggest that parents *remove your children immediately* from this organization as well as your support from the United Way, and all other businesses that fund them. Listen carefully!

The homosexuals do not understand what they are doing because it is a spiritual and moral issue. The unsaved person, *under the control of his sin nature,* may become hostile, demonstrating hatred toward God, and the things of God. He is at enmity, or an enemy of God (Romans 8:7). And as a result, *our truth may seem evil to them.* It is only *natural* for the unsaved mind to *show hatred and hostility at times toward those who disagree with them.* Listen again to what God says about these people in 2 Peter 2:12, "But these… speak evil of the things that they understand not; and shall utterly perish in their own corruption." That is quite a statement from God our Creator. While many homosexuals are perishing in their *own* corruption, they may demonstrate hostility and hatred by actively brutalizing and at times, murdering innocent people.

Case in point: Awhile back in the state of Arkansas, Joshua McCave Brown, a homosexual, sodomized Jesse Dirkhising, a 13-year old boy. Brown and his lover David Carpenter brutally beat and murdered Jesse Dirkhising by strangling him with his own underwear.[3] This is just part of their confession. Most of the liberal news media did not cover this story. They refused to do it and it was hidden from the majority of Americans. One station dared to air the news story, but after that, **received death threats from the gay activists.** Again, if **their lifestyle were as they say, "natural healthy acts of love," then why would they commit murder and send out death threats?** My friend, this is a **real hate crime from the homosexuals.**

Yes, this so-called "Non Discrimination Bill," or "Hate Crimes Bill" will be forced upon our nation so we can no longer speak out against this evil. Let us not allow it to happen. Folks, this should be reversed! The "Hate Crimes Bill" should be directed toward the homosexuals. **Listen carefully with your heart, dear friend, for it is not a crime to hate sin, but it is a serious hate crime to promote and force sins upon a society that opposes it.** A number of states may have passed this bill, including New York, and it was about to be passed in Maryland; but before this happened a Republican won the governorship. What do you think of that, my friend?

*The gay agenda together with the "Hate Crimes Bill" would give homosexuals the **same rights traditional families** have, such as tax breaks, adoption of children, and marriage rights. At the same time, homosexuals are going to the high courts to coerce the Supreme Court judges to include same sex marriages along with our moral traditional marriages. Satan's purpose is to destroy what God has created or put together—the natural traditional families in America.* My friend, *sin does not have any rights.* Let me repeat myself: sinful perverted behavior does not have any rights. **The only right the homosexuals and lesbians have in God's eyes is to repent.**

I hasten to clarify myself by saying that homosexuals as individual persons have the same rights as the rest of us as long as they keep their behavior problems to themselves. *But, they do not have the right to force a society to accept their perverted sin as normal and healthy, nor force judges to rewrite the constitute for perverted marriages. This is when their rights stop and the rights of decent people overrule them. Frankly,* their acts of behavior should be disgusting and embarrassing to a normal, moral society and nation.

Again to re-emphasize what I have said previously, but in a different way: God created Adam and Eve, a man and woman, not Adam and John. God took a rib from Adam and formed the woman. Therefore, a woman is "naturally (genetically) attracted" to the man, or drawn "naturally to the man and vice versa." Why is this, or what was God's purpose for creating opposite sexes? Obviously, it was to begin the human race *by producing children.* If God had intended to produce a homosexual race, then He would have "equipped" man with man to produce children! But He did not. Can homosexuals produce children between the two of them? NO! Even animals know the difference. *God has put within humans and animals natural instincts of what is natural behavior.*

Listen once more to Romans 1:26-27,

> *"For this cause, God gave them up unto vile affections: for even their women did change the natural use into that which is against nature. And likewise also the men leaving the natural use of the woman, burned in their lust one toward another, men with men working that which is unseemly, and receiving in themselves that recompense of their error."*

And, in 1 Corinthians 6:9-10,

> *"Know ye not that the unrighteous shall not inherit the kingdom of God? Be not deceived: neither fornicators, nor idolaters, nor adulterers, nor effeminate, nor abusers of themselves with mankind, [homosexuals] nor thieves, nor drunkards, nor revilers, nor extortioners,* shall inherit the kingdom of God."

Dear homosexual friend, it is *very, very dangerous to continue in your sin,* for God said that He "gave them up." This is a terrible thing to know when you are practicing this sin. I believe without a doubt that these are the most tragic words

God could ever say to people. *I strongly urge of you to ask God to forgive you, and invite Jesus Christ to come into your heart and save you before it is eternally too late for your eternal soul.* We are allowing ourselves to be incredibly blinded and deceived by Satan's lies. We are without excuse. Sin reacts like cancer, in that it does not care who it destroys. I make no apology for repeating myself, by saying the same things in different ways; this is to get your attention, folks, to see the urgency and criticalness of our situation.

A great number of homosexuals are now called "activists," and **one of their major goals is to take over and control America by getting to our children, so the next generation will be mostly homosexuals, resulting in our nation becoming Sodom and Gomorrah.** And, it looks like they are in the process of doing it, because their fourth goal was to infiltrate the school education system and add the homosexual lifestyle to the curriculum. This includes homosexual teachers teaching our young children their abominable behavior is good and healthy. This is being done in California, and more recently in Broward County, Florida. Former Governor Gray Davis of California signed a bill to require it in public schools. *This is how they are forcing this sinful behavior upon our society and nation* by getting people who control the school system teamed up with political figures to force control of America.

Do you not see what is taking place, folks? *The homosexuals are an army of immoral terrorist activists, who are invading our nation and striking in crucial areas at the same time with great impact, such as the educational system, the Hollywood system, the political system, the godly traditional family system, the religious system, and the business system. And as a result, our nation is at this very moment helplessly crippled, and multitudes of Americans do not realize what is taking place.* **Folks, they will stop at nothing to achieve their goal, even murder, which you may not hear about in the main news media.

As I have mentioned above, the homosexuals have for a number of years been gaining tremendous numbers of supporters from the Hollywood crowd. A large number of big-time supporters in Hollywood are pushing and slowly presenting the wicked homosexual lifestyle as normal and acceptable through the TV and movie media. And, we are allowing our children and teenagers as well as ourselves to watch these immoral programs at the movies and on TV. No wonder our nation is so corrupt. This is part of the homosexual goals. Jeremiah 4:22 says, "They are wise to do evil, but to do good they have no knowledge."

Let us take a look at some figures: There are approximately 280 million people in America, and out of that figure, how many are homosexuals and lesbians? In a poll taken in 1990, there were only at most 2 percent homosexuals,[4] and I will give the homosexuals the benefit of the doubt by assuming the 2 percent did not include lesbians. If you add the author's guess of another 2 percent for lesbians, there may have been about 4 percent total, or 11.2 million. But, if we update these figures for today, the author projects a generous total figure of 6 percent, or 16.8 million. One may say, "Well that is not very many out of 280 million, nothing to get alarmed over." I say, "Reread what I have just said above about the impact the homosexuals have made on this nation." Listen to the following statement: In year 2001, a poll was reported by SRN news on Christian radio that the percentage of Americans who considered the homosexual and lesbian "lifestyle" to be acceptable was 51 percent. My *friend, this is a staggering percentage.* If the homosexuals and lesbians were not included in the percentage, then 143 million people, including sympathizers, have accepted, or are tolerating the homosexual lifestyle.

Therefore, they are not going to take a stand or get involved against this wickedness. Again, this shows what kind of impact 4 percent or 6 percent has on America! This also seems to be an encouragement, or open door if you will, for the homosexual and lesbian activists to continue pressing on to further establish their beachhead and invasion agenda.

In order to spread their wickedness, they go after big influential people in the Congress and Senate. They also seek weak-minded homosexual sympathizers as a former Governor of California and a former Governor of Maryland, as well as most of the Hollywood crowd. Do you suppose there were 143 million in the cities of Sodom and Gomorrah when God destroyed these cities? I say no. What about 1 million, or 100 thousand? Probably not; but 143 million means that all these may as well be homosexuals and lesbians because they are on their side. And if nothing is done about it, they too will soon be just like them, because they tolerate and accept what the homosexuals are doing. *Is this the way we want American to end?*

I dare say that more than the majority of these people do not even know the agenda of the homosexuals. And even if they were aware of their agenda, would they respond and oppose them? A great number of Americans play ignorant and live in their own small little world, and therefore do not get involved in any controversial situations. *This should not be controversial, but we have allowed it to happen by doing nothing!* These are some of the reasons why the homosexuals have established a beachhead in America.

Friend, *not understanding and not wanting to get involved are destructive to any nation.* Are we going to allow these homosexuals to intimidate and deceive our nation so that we will not speak out against their sin? Make no mistake about it friend, this agenda is causing destruction within America. Remember my comparison of the small cities of Sodom and

Gomorrah to cities of America? *If God destroyed those cities in that small land of Israel,* **how much more** *wickedness will God allow before He decides to destroy our entire nation? I can tell you when this will happen, and that is when they take over the leadership and businesses of this nation!* **It has been said,** "History repeats itself." **Just as God destroyed Sodom and Gomorrah, America is quickly rushing to that disastrous end.** Remember 2 Peter 2:6,

> "*And turning the cities of Sodom and Gomorrha into ashes condemned them with an overthrow,* **making them an ensample unto those that after should live ungodly.**"

Do you want this to happen? You say, "No," and I say, "Now that we really know what is taking place, what are we going to do about it?" Dearly beloved, do not let it happen to our great nation. Again, I say, "The hour is late for America. *Our condition is beyond critical, worse than Sodom and Gomorrah.*" *Where are those who are standing in the GAP?*

There are some people who are taking a stand and these are, of all people, **ex-homosexuals and lesbians. Yes, former homosexuals and lesbians have come out of the homosexual lifestyle of sin.** I have heard the testimony of a married couple, man and wife, **former homosexual and lesbian** now living normal lives **and serving the Lord.** What an amazing work of God's grace and mercy! They have been saved by the grace of God, and I have one couple's life story on tape and in a book.[5] We may never hear about these who have come out of that lifestyle on the liberal news media. *That is bias and hate, friend*! You have to tune into Christian radio and hear Christian conservative programming with news from a Christian perspective to really find out what is going on in America. Homosexuals not only try to destroy and discredit the testimonies of these who have been saved by the grace of God, but now they are persecuting former homosexuals. This is a demonstration of hate from the homosexuals. Again we see who are the real haters. **If these dear people can take their stand, how much more should we be making up the hedge, standing in the gap, and warning these activists of the danger ahead!**

There are some taking a stand for God and country, but just a few. God has His remnant, and I know a few of them. The ones I know about, I support financially and in prayer. Again, this is a spiritual battle. It is a battle for our minds. God says to the Christian in Ephesians 6:10-17,

> "Finally my brethren, be strong in the Lord, and in the power of his might. Put on the whole armour of God, that ye may be able to stand against the wiles of the devil. For we wrestle not against flesh and blood, but against principalities, against the rulers of the darkness of this world, against spiritual wickedness in high places. Wherefore take unto you the whole armour of God, that ye may be able to withstand in the evil day, and having done all, to stand. Stand therefore having your loins girt about with the truth, and having on the breastplate of righteousness; And your feet shod with the preparation of the gospel of peace; Above all, taking the shield of faith, wherewith ye are able to quench all the fiery darts of the wicked. And take the helmet of salvation, and the sword of the Spirit, which is the word of God."

What a demanding and critical command from God in these critical days in which we are living—"having done all, to stand."

According to God's timetable, Satan knows his time is short, and his end is coming when he will be cast in the lake of fire. Therefore, he is going all out to deceive as many as he can to join him in the lake of fire (Revelation 20:10-15). *Spiritual warfare is the game!* I will come back to this subject later on and show in another way just how our condition is beyond the critical point in the "**game of life or death.**" This is just one of the many horses of Satan that is out there deceiving and destroying America.

Let us look at another horse, which is one of Satan's greatest devouring deceptions for the destruction of little bodies and our moral society.

2. Abortion

Yes, I am going to talk about this so-called very controversial subject. If I were to ask for hands of those who believe that there is nothing wrong with abortion, how many raised hands would I see across America? Well, I am not going to ask for hands, because I already have a good idea. But when this section is concluded, I trust there would not be one hand raised.

First of all, I shall begin with a statement that should not be controversial: I believe a *person's life begins at conception.* Do not be deceived by Satan, dear friend. Make no mistake about it, **that baby, that person in that mother's womb is a human being.** And where there is movement and swelling in the womb, there is life, a life of a human being.

Listen carefully to the following words of God:

> "I was cast upon thee from the womb: thou art my God from my mother's belly" (Psalm 22:10).

> "Thou hast covered me in my mother's womb" (Psalm 139:13).

> "How the bones do grow in the womb of her that is with child" (Ecclesiastes 11:5).

"Thus saith the Lord that made me, and formed me from the womb" (Isaiah 44:2)

"The Lord that formed me from the womb to be his servant" (Isaiah 49:5)

and in Isaiah 49:15

"Can a woman forget her sucking child that she should not have compassion on the son of her womb? yea, they may forget, yet will I not forget thee."

Whom should we believe—God our Creator, or Satan, the author of lies? God says, "Let God be true and every man a liar" (Romans 3:4), "God that cannot lie" (Titus 1:2), and it is "impossible for God to lie" (Hebrews 6:18).

A great number of people do not believe God, or do not believe there is a God; therefore, their unbelief gives them an excuse to do whatever they want! That is why it is controversial, but it should not be, because unbelief does not change the reality of the existence of God. So, why would we lie to ourselves and deceive ourselves? The answer is simple—LUST. We want to keep on enjoying our sin regardless of right or wrong even if it means the murder of unwanted innocent babies. Do not be deceived by Satan's lies. Are you one that is being deceived? Dear friend, life begins at conception.

Secondly, a*bortion is murder!* The "Women's Lib" movement has deceived millions upon millions of young girls and older women into committing murder. The abortion (murder clinics) people are taking advantage of poor deceived women and girls, as a "money-making" industry, to get rich from the mass murder of innocent babies, who cannot defend themselves. *It should not be "God Bless America!" God has blessed America all these years and still blessing our nation; but now we* *should be on our knees asking God to forgive us for our sins. May 2 Chronicles 7:14 be our cry to God as a nation!*

There is a video called *Baby Parts* [6] that graphically shows the horrors and atrocities of abortion murder, as well as *the selling of the baby parts for profit*. Viewing this film will change your thinking if you are a human being. But you say, "I do not accept all that; I can do whatever I want with my body; after all it is my body."

Well, let us look at that statement: First of all, that statement did not *originate* from you, but it came from others on down the line from its source—Satan himself. Secondly, you gave your body over to your boy friend to get you pregnant, so he then has equal rights to "your body" and your baby. He has every right to decide what to do as well as you. Think about that. Thirdly, you say your body belongs to you. Well I say, "On the authority of God's Word, your body does not belong to you, but to God." The body you are walking around in has been loaned to you to house your spirit which is of God. God created us out of the dust of the ground. We are His creation, and one of these days we will give up this body in death and it goes back to dust—"for dust thou art, and unto dust shalt thou return" (Genesis 3:19).

Allow me to ask you these questions: "Did you have anything to do with your creation? Did Adam and Eve have anything to do with their creation?" The answer is NO. Therefore, does it make any sense to say, "Our body is our body to do whatever we want with it!" Again, God loaned us a body to house our spirit. Everything we see and do not see belongs to God our Creator. If we abuse what belongs to God, then we will not only have to stand one day before God and be accountable, but before that day, we will reap what we have sown in the body. God says,

> *"Be not deceived; God is not mocked: for whatsoever a man soweth, that shall he also reap. For he that*

soweth to the flesh shall also of the flesh reap corruption" (Galatians 6:7-8).

And, that is a promise from God, for it is one of God's laws.

We wonder why these bodies are afflicted with AIDS, and children are born with AIDS and other sexual diseases. We are His creation, my friend. We have a spirit and as such we are spirit beings as well as physical beings. Listen to the rest of Galatians 6:8, "But he that soweth to the Spirit shall of the Spirit reap life everlasting." This is talking about God's Spirit, not ours.

Let us read what God says about how we are to use the bodies He has loaned to us:

> "What? Know ye not that your body is the temple of the Holy Spirit which is in you, which ye have of God, and ye are not your own? For ye are bought with a price: therefore glorify God in your body, and in your spirit, which are God's" (1 Corinthians 6:19-20).

Whether you are a Christian or non-Christian, you should honor God with these bodies of His.

I believe abortion is murder except to save the mother's life. The courts declared way back in 1973 in the *Roe v. Wade* case that the fetus in the mother's womb was not human. So, the baby is now called a fetus, because they do not want to say "baby, child, or a person" because the court's ruled "not human." As a result of the courts decision, since *Roe v. Wade*, forty million plus **human beings** have been butchered and murdered. Hitler's legalist said the same thing, that the Jews were not human; consequently, Hitler murdered six million **human beings**.

Beloved, *think carefully about these thoughts:* Some time ago, the eyes and ears of our nation and around the world were glued to the TV and radio when nine coal miners were *trapped and completely helpless* 240 feet *beneath the earth in a dark air pocket in a coal mine* in Somerset, PA. Multitudes of people were gathered together anxiously waiting and praying to God that the miners might be saved from certain death. The expert rescuers drilled an airshaft for the miners to breathe and another one to rescue the miners. God heard the prayers of the people and the miners were safely *delivered out of their trapped and helpless situation*. But, suppose the expert rescuers, instead of delivering the miners safely out of their trapped tiny air pocket, pumped cyanide gas into the rescue shaft and murdered them! We would be shocked and outraged, calling that the most brutal, savage murder ever witnessed, and rightly so.

But, we Americans are witnessing that very same thing every day with a little *live human being, trapped and completely helpless in a tiny air pocket called the woman's womb*. Instead of the *expert rescuers delivering the little trapped and helpless baby out of that womb*, they butcher and murder the baby. Or, while they are bringing the baby halfway out of the "shaft," the birth canal, they have a hole drilled in its head to suck the brains out, thus murdering the helpless baby. Then, they dismember the baby parts and sell them for profit.[7] How *barbaric and brutal* can a "person" be, dear friend! Where are all the eyes of Americans who know about these *ongoing atrocities* but are not speaking out?

Heaven has and is being populated with forty million babies, and at the same time, hell is and will be populated with forty million mothers and abortionist butchers, if they do not repent of their sin and ask Jesus to save them. Many have turned to God and their lives have been changed. But, multitudes of people who murdered their children may well spend eternity in torment in the flames of hell, if there is no repentance! *So I say to America that the sin of abortion murder is greater than Hitler's atrocities. May God have mercy on our nation!* Friend, again *think carefully about this*: I believe all the babies that have been murdered are in the very presence of Jesus. And just suppose that these little ones will be with Jesus at the Great White Throne Judgment of God, just to point their fingers at their unsaved mothers and abortionists and say, *"You murdered me!"* What a sobering, eye-opening thought.

Dear friend, if you are thinking of aborting your baby, *think again.* You may not get the death penalty on earth, but I guarantee you will get it when you stand before God, Revelation 20:11-15. The only way to escape eternal conscious torment is to get the victory over the footman of the flesh by becoming a born-again Christian. If you murdered your baby through abortion, God will forgive you. You must repent of your sin of unbelief and this atrocious sin, and receive Jesus Christ into your heart as Savior and Lord of your life. God then saves you, forgives you, and makes you a child of His. *That is a promise from God's Word, and your baby will forgive you.* I trust you will do it now before it is eternally too late. May God help you to respond to God's Word! **Friend, do not let lust destroy you and the body that God has loaned you.** God is looking for women and girls to take a stand. Speak out against this giant horse, get the victory, and put the abortionist crowd out of business *before God's wrath is poured out on America.* Will you be one who will take a stand for God and against the abortionist horse?

The next horses in society are the *intermediate causes of abortion* and they are:

3. Fornication and Adultery

Fornication and adultery may seem to be foreign words to most of our young people today, and maybe it is because they have never heard these words until now. For the past number of years, all we heard was "safe sex," and our young people were given condoms like candy, which did not solve the problem, only encouraged them to continue. Then more recently, we have been telling our young people to "abstain from sex," or "just say no." Friend, that is almost impossible, because we have made it an acceptable lifestyle; boys and girls, men and women are going to have sex anyway, or not fit in with their peer groups. "Abstain from sex"—what kind of statement is this? What do we mean when we say *abstain*? This is what it may mean to a teen—Ok, I will abstain from sex for one day, or maybe one week, or one hour! It is like waving candy in front of a baby and saying you cannot eat—nonsense!

And, now we have another somewhat foolish statement, "Abstinence till after marriage." The reason why I say what I say is because the statements are meaningless! That is, it is not good enough, it does not go far enough, and the answer from numerous teens and young men and women to all these good sounding phrases and having babies is a big "**So what!**"

Dear friend, something very important is missing from all these statements and it is the *why* or the *reason* behind these statements. We cannot say, "Do not do this or that" without a WHY or REASON for being so negative. Oh yes, we do give a reason by saying, "You may catch AIDS or other diseases," or in the one case above, "Till you get married." This is important, but again, it is not good enough. And, the big why and reason is one three-letter word—*SIN*. God says, "It is sin." Our young people are listening to the wrong voices that say, "Everybody is doing it; it is alright to have fun; feed and explore your sexual appetite, and feel the excitement; surrender to your fleshy footman, after all your friends are doing it, and it is all over TV and the movies." Therefore, our young people conclude that it must be OK!

Friends, parents, we had better listen to God, our Creator instead of the lies of Satan and his crowd. **Having sex apart** from marriage is *sin*, and it is called *fornication*. **Marriage is the *only* acceptable time for sex.** In Genesis 2:21-25 God tells us that after He created Adam, He then caused Adam to sleep while He took a rib from him to form a woman and brought her to Adam to be *his wife*. It was God who performed the first marriage, and by the way it was between man and woman, not between man and man. After Adam and Eve were married, God said, "And they were both naked, <u>the man and his wife</u>, and were *not ashamed*." I underscored man and his wife to emphasize that sex outside of marriage brings *shame, disgrace, and disrespect for one another*. Later on God said in Genesis 4:1, "And Adam knew Eve his wife and she conceived, and bare Cain." Notice, Eve is Adam's wife. The word *knew* means sexual relations. **This is the only acceptable sexual relationship between male and female—a***ny other relationship is sin.*

Two of the most damaging and destructive horses running loose in America without any restraints from society are the sins of fornication and adultery. And if we cannot get the victory over self, our fleshy footmen, then how in the world are we going to run against these horses? For those of you who do not know the difference between adultery and fornication, allow me to reemphasize and define these terms: Adultery is immoral sexual relations of married couples outside their marriage bonds. Look up these words in your dictionary. Fornication refers to many sexual sins and often refers to immoral sexual relations between unmarried couples (male and female). One of the Ten Commandments is "Thou shalt not commit adultery."

For some of you, this is the first time you have heard that sex outside of marriage is sin, and married couples having sex with others is sin. But I hasten to say, that if you are a normal person, your conscience will tell you it is **wrong. And, that is the way God made us.** Do not be deceived by the so-called "safe sex" flag, for there is no safe sex outside marriage in God's eyes. Safe sex does not take care of the matter. *Only in marriage will there be safety.*

Hebrews 13:4 says,

> "Marriage is honourable in all and the bed undefiled: but whoremongers and adulterers God will judge."

Those who are having sex outside of marriage are called "whoremongers." I want to repeat what God also says in Galatians 6:7-8, "Be not deceived; God is not mocked: for whatsoever a man soweth, that shall he reap. For he that soweth to his flesh shall reap corruption; but he that soweth to the Spirit shall of the Spirit reap life everlasting." Sin is not free. It is very costly. It takes its toll on the body with sickness and disease that oftentimes will destroy the body.

Our nation seems to think that fornication and adultery is an acceptable lifestyle. We have adulterers and fornicators living together. They call it a "live-in friend," or unmarried cohabitation these days—the "in thing." "By 2000 the total number of unmarried couples in America was almost four and three-quarters million, up from less than half a million in 1960.... Over half of all first marriages are now preceded by cohabitation, compared to virtually none earlier in the century."[8]

Living together outside of marriage is a popular thing today, especially when "in recent national surveys nearly 66 percent of high school senior boys and 61 percent of girls indicated that they 'agreed' or 'mostly agreed' with the statement 'it is usually a good idea for a couple to live together before getting married in order to find out whether they really get along' ....The new view is that cohabitation represents a more progressive approach to intimate relationships. How much healthier women are to be free of social pressure to marry and stigma when they do not. How much better off people are today to be able to exercise choice in their sexual and domestic arrangements. How much better off marriages can be, and how many divorces can be avoided, when relationships start with a trial period....If it does not work out, one can simply move out. According to this reasoning, cohabitation weeds out unsuitable partners through a process of natural de-selection."[9] *However*, "much of the accumulating social science research suggest otherwise....Cohabitation does not reduce the likelihood of eventual divorce; in fact, it is associated with a higher divorce risk...the chances of divorce ending a marriage preceded by cohabitation are significantly greater than for a marriage not preceded by cohabitation.... And no positive contribution of cohabitation to marriage has been found."[10] Wow, we can see by all of this that multitudes of parents, our public schools, colleges, and universities of "higher learning" are a tragic failure in teaching moral values to our young people.

Dear friend, if you are in a situation like the above, or thinking about it, listen very carefully to these words of admonition and warnings: In the above cohabitation arrangements, I see a few things lacking, which are the true ingredients of a lasting marriage relationship; namely, *true love, commitment, honor, and respect.* True love is the only kind of love that will last and keep a marriage together in good times as well as bad times. It will not be shaken when disappointments come, and believe me they will come, but true love can get the victory. True love is the key to the beginning of one of the greatest exciting adventures in life for a man and a woman.

When I say true love, I mean a love that is different from a love that you would have for your parents, your friends or group of friends, animals, your job or car. True love is when a man and woman fall *in love* with each other so much so that they become part of each other and cannot stand being without each other's company for one moment. The couple is totally *committed* to each other, having the same mind about most things, complementing, *honoring* and *respecting* one another in thought and desires. Both share the same dream and goal of being with each other the rest of their lives so much so that they want to get married as soon as possible. This *kind of love, commitment, honor, and respect for each other will wait till marriage before intimate sexual love is experienced between one another.* And when this happens, the two become truly one, lost in each other's love until death parts them. And, I hasten to say that if this couple are truly born-again Christians, they possess the very love of God in their hearts, and that their love for each other is encased in God's love for all eternity. Commitment, honor, and respect are products of true love.

Dear friend, you can count on this kind of love relationship to keep a marriage together in an overwhelming majority of cases. This kind of love marriage is what is lacking in most marriages today, and why multitudes of marriages are failing. Multitudes of marriages are based on a friendship kind of love, even though they may honor and respect each other, their marriage will in all probability fail. So then, what multitudes of couples believe to be love is nothing but lust, *selfish sexual lust.* Thus we have cohabitation between unmarried couples, an excuse to lust from one person to another, with no commitment, respect, or honor for each other, more so with men than women.

Again, while cohabilitation may be popular and cute in the eyes of society, it is wickedness *in God's eyes.* I said, "in God's eyes" because He is there present with you. One of God's attributes is being omnipresent, which means God is everywhere present, and though cohabitation may not get much outrage from society, God sees all and is keeping the records.

Friend, we cannot hide from God. He is everywhere we are, and He is going to hold us accountable for what we do with the bodies He has entrusted to us. May God help us to see this great truth, and flee from a sinful relationship to God for forgiveness and salvation!

Question? When have you heard a sermon on the sins of adultery and fornication? You say once or twice, or maybe never! This may be the case, if you are a teen, or a young man or woman who never goes to church, or goes to modernistic liberal churches. If you *never hear* about these and others sins from the pulpits, *or never read God's Instruction Book, then you will think it is all right to practice fornication and adultery. Rise up pastors, teachers, and make up a hedge of righteousness, stand in the gap, and run with the footmen and horses!* You will not lose your flock, but God will honor your stand and increase your listening audience. America's young people inwardly are desperately crying out to hear the truth.

What are the results or effects of adultery and fornication, in most cases? **Unwanted babies** and **abortion!** The baby is viewed as a nuisance and is in the way of having fun. No wonder we have allowed forty **million babies** to be **murdered in America**. And no one is raising the red flag and saying, "*Enough is enough. It is sin!*" *Dear friend, we reap what we sow, good or bad.* No wonder AIDS is spreading like a prairie fire. *This is part of God's judgment.* Oh, you may get by with it for awhile, but suddenly you are stricken with AIDS, gonorrhea, and death. God's law says this, "The wages of sin is death" (Romans 6:23).

The movie and TV industry promotes unmarried immoral sexual relationships among young people as glamorous and the normal way of living, including divorce and remarriage. These sins, including divorce and remarriage, are exploding in our nation. Even though society says this is acceptable, God sees it differently—He says there is but one reason for divorce and He mentions it in Matthew 5:32. "Whosoever shall put away his wife, saving for the cause of fornication, causes her to commit adultery: and whosoever shall marry her that is divorced committeth adultery" (*put away* means divorce). *Marriage is till death do us part*, and it does not matter how many times one divorces and remarries, it is still living in adultery (Romans 7:2-3). It is a lifelong commitment, friend. Satan is so **deceptive** and yet, he does not have to **deceive** us much at times to get us to believe his lies.

The satanic spirit of the movie and TV industry does not dare show the other side of glamorizing sin—sorrow, murder, destruction, ruined lives, diseased lives, death, and the murder of innocent babies. The sin of fornication often produces murder through abortion. Again I say, "*We reap what we sow.*" I want to quickly state that just because you say, "I did not know that all these are sins," does not excuse you. God has placed within your being a little mechanism called your conscience that whispers to you that you should not do this or that as well as approves. Therefore, you are without excuse and responsible, and God will hold you accountable for your sin. Romans 2:15 says,

> "*The work of the law written in their hearts, their conscience also bearing witness, and their thoughts the mean while accusing or else excusing one another.*"

For the Christian a warning! 1 Corinthians 6:18-20 says,

> "*Flee fornication. Every sin that a man doeth is without the body; but he that committed fornication sinneth against his own body. What? Know ye not that your body is the temple of the Holy Ghost which is in you, which ye have of God, and ye are not your own?*

> *For ye are brought with a price: therefore glorify God in your body, and in your spirit, which are God's."*

Again, God gives another warning in 1 Corinthians 6:9-10,

> *"Know ye not that the unrighteous shall not inherit the kingdom of God? Be not deceived: neither fornicators, nor idolaters, nor adulterers, nor effeminate, nor abusers of themselves with mankind [homosexuals], nor thieves, nor drunkards, nor revilers, nor extortioners, shall inherit the kingdom of God."*

God lists a lot of sins, and fornication and adultery is among these sins. God is saying that those who *practice a lifestyle of these sins and die without Christ will not go to heaven.* In Galatians 5:19-21, notice these same sins are listed again as well as others:

> *"Now the works of the flesh are manifest, which are these: Adultery, fornication, uncleanness, lasciviousness, idolatry, witchcraft, hatred, variance, emulations, wrath, strife, seditions, heresies, envyings, murders, drunkenness, revellings, and such like; as I have also told you in time past, that they which do such things shall not inherit the kingdom of God."*

Now we have arrived at a point where I want to again deal with our number-one enemy the flesh, or self. It is important for us to understand the kind of enemy we are facing. What do you notice in the previous verses? You see the word *flesh*. Reread and think about what the verse is saying—"Now the works of the flesh are manifest, which are these:" A list follows of the "works" or sins. Listen very carefully when I say, "Those sins listed above are some of the horses running loose in America." I only mentioned three of them in this chapter—adultery, fornication, and the sin of the homosexuals. I also touched on hatred in my discussion of homosexuals. But, I want us to notice that these horses come from our flesh. They are a manifestation of our flesh. In other words, these sins lie dormant in our flesh until we yield to our fleshly desires and the temptations of Satan, then we give birth to them and we become part of the horses that are destroying our nation. Think about what I just said! Instead of making up the hedge and standing in the gap, we can become part of the gigantic horses ourselves. Friend, this is so important that we understand our number-one enemy, the flesh.

Notice the little word *do* in the above verses. This means to make these sins a **practice** in your life. Again, in Revelation 21:8, God calls fornicators and adulterers "whoremongers," and He goes on to say that whoremongers along with other sinful behavior such as "the fearful, and unbelieving, and the abominable, murderers, and sorcerers, and idolaters, and all liars, *shall have their part in the lake which burneth with fire and brimstone: which is the second death."* What an awful destination awaits those who live in their sin, or their lifestyle is the practice of these sins, for they are racing toward their own destructive destruction. May God help us to see how critical and short our life may be on planet Earth and our need to come face to face with our sin before it is too late!

Can you not see the adultery, fornication, and abortion horses destroying our nation as well as the other horses that go along with these, such as the Internet and TV pornography in our homes, and in our public libraries? What are you going to do about it? *If we stop the sins of fornication, adultery and pornography, we stop the sin of abortion, and we run the abortionist murderers out of business.*

Will you, dear friend, be one who will be part of the hedge and stand in the gap, take a stand against these horses and run with them to stop this destruction of *yourself and our society? It takes courage to go against peer pressure, and the flood of wickedness, but God is looking for brave young men and women* **to do** *that very thing.*

Parents, be part of the hedge by teaching your children moral values as they grow up. Teach them to respect themselves and others. Your children are desperately crying out for boundaries and guidelines. Spend time with your children. Of course, if you as parents are living in sin yourselves and being destroyed by these horses, then your children will follow in your footsteps.

God says,

> *"I sought for a man among them, that should make up the hedge, and stand in the gap before me for the land, that I should not destroy it: but I found none"* (Ezekiel 22:30).

What *tragic* and *sad* words—"but I found none."

Who will take a stand against fornication and adultery, and all the rest of the wickedness I am mentioning in this message, and make up a hedge for God and America? Will you speak out? Minister, will you speak out and warn your flock about the footman of the flesh and these horses, or will you let your flock live in sin, so you can keep your "job" and your congregation? Are we going to obey Satan or God? You cannot do both!

Again, Jesus said, "He that is not with me is against me" (Mathew 12:30). Whosoever keeps their mouth shut and does not speak out on these issues is a vote for wickedness, and is an enemy of God. Think about that, and then think about this: Satan is using his horses of fornication and adultery, abortion, homosexuality, and pornography to destroy America's traditional family structure.

The Means by Which Satan Is Destroying America

Our family structure is eroding away and declining at a rapid pace in our nation as shown in the following report: "According to the U.S. Census Bureau May 15, 2001, the 1990s saw a marked increase in every kind of household, except one; the traditional two-parent family....The data from that year's census showed that married couples, with or without children, comprise a lower percentage of American households than ever before. In fact, people living alone outnumber traditional 'married-with-children' families."[11]

Satan is attacking the traditional family unit, because God started the family as we understand from the book of Genesis:

> *"And the Lord God caused a deep sleep to fall upon Adam, and he slept: and he took one of his ribs, and closed up the flesh instead thereof; and the rib, which the Lord God had taken from man, made he a woman, and brought her unto the man. And Adam said, This is now bone of my bones, and flesh of my flesh: she shall be called Woman, because she was taken out of Man. Therefore shall a man leave his father and mother, and shall cleave unto his wife: and they shall be one flesh"* (Genesis 2:21-24).

> *"So God created man in his own image, in the image of God created he him; male and female created he them. And God blessed them, and God said unto them, Be fruitful and multiply, and replenish the earth,..."* (Genesis 1:27-28).

Americans, we must maintain our Biblical family structure. **Who is going to take a stand for the American family? Can God count on you?**

Let us turn our attention, and I do mean your attention to another sinister and festering monster horse that is out to destroy our young children, so that the next generation will know nothing about the traditional family values. Let us look at the fourth horse that is targeting our public school system, and that is the organization called the National Educational Association (NEA):

4. The National Educational Association (NEA)

I want to make a statement at the beginning of this section that may alarm some parents: The NEA mostly controls and *funds everything except proper education* in our public school system. The following information is taken from the booklet "Grading the NEA: A Special Report" by Perry L. Glanzer, Ph.D. and Travis R. Pardo, and published by Focus on the Family. Please pay close attention to where your money is distributed and the kind of education your children are being exposed to at a very early age.

> "The National Education Association (NEA) is one of the nation's largest and most powerful unions. Its 2.5 million members comprise more than half of the public school teachers in the United States...it receives nearly $1 billion in estimated annual revenues. With such a vast membership and enormous financial support, the NEA is the single most powerful force in education.... Many might be surprised to know that their money is spent by the NEA to promote an agenda that conflicts with some of their most deeply held moral and religious beliefs. ...To understand the NEA's views, we turn to a list of official resolutions...or position of the Association.
>
> a. Supporting 'Reproductive Freedom,' ...includes a woman's right to have an abortion.

b. The Promotion of Homosexuality, Bisexuality and Transgenderism, ...in a Phi Delta Kappa/Gallup poll, 63 percent of the public opposed 'teaching about the gay and lesbian lifestyle as part of the curriculum in the public schools' in their community. Furthermore, 'if teaching about the gay and lesbian lifestyle were included in the curriculum of the local public schools,' only 9 percent believe it should be presented as 'an acceptable alternate lifestyle.' ...NEA President Bob Chase offered a strong endorsement of a pro-homosexual video for students entitled It's Elementary: Talking About Gay Issues in School. Chase stated, 'Schools cannot be neutral when we're dealing with [homosexual] issues.... I'm not talking about tolerance. I'm talking about acceptance...'

c. Opposing Parental Choice. The NEA resolutions also take strong stands against several educational options that give more power and responsibility to parents: 'Home Schooling,' 'Parental Optional Plans,' and 'Vouchers and tax credits.'

d. Teaching Educators to Fight Conservative Religious Groups and Parents. One NEA resolution...condemns...what they call 'the radical right,' 'the extreme right,'....
The NEA specifically warns against groups such as Concerned Women for America, Eagle Forum, Family Research Council, Christian Coalition, American Family Association, Focus on the Family, and the Traditional Values Coalition. According to the NEA, these groups 'aggressive campaigns, large followings, and strong-arm tactics divide communities and disrupt the work of the public schools....'
During the 1990s, recipients of NEA financial support included the pro-abortion National

Organization for Women (NOW), the pro-homosexual Gay & lesbian Alliance Against Defamation and the Human Rights Campaign Fund, and People for the American Way (PAW), an organization that attacks conservative Christian groups. PAW has received an astounding $654,000 from the NEA in the past decade.... The election of 1998.... The NEA ranked as the third-largest contributor to political candidates and organizations in the entire nation.... Of the NEA's $3.4 million contribution, 95 percent went to Democrats and 5 percent to Republicans. Furthermore, a 1999 Fortune magazine survey ranked the NEA ninth among the 114 most powerful lobbying groups in Washington, DC.... Although only 49 percent of NEA members claim affiliation with the Democratic Party, that is the party to which the vast majority of the NEA's political funding is given.... During the 1998 elections, the NEA Fund for Children and Public Education.... Of the $2.2 million contributed, 93 percent went to Democrats and 7 percent to Republicans."[12]

Parents, teachers, and friends, we can sadly see throughout the NEA Agenda where most of your funds are going politically and socially, as well as fighting opposition from Conservative Religious Groups and Parents. Again, these are the ones the NEA calls "extremist" and "the radical right."

I believe the reason for this strong opposition is because the NEA wants the control of our children in order to corrupt their minds. **They do this by taking advantage of parents, knowing that parents believe that their children will be taught the right things in the public schools.**

Folks, it appears that many in the NEA leadership are anti-God, anti-Christ, anti-morals, and socialistic, left-wing liberals. It also appears that most of the NEA leadership are so willingly blinded that they think they are doing the right thing, and do not realize what they are doing to our children, our families, our society, and our nation. This is incredible blindness. **Where is the outrage, friends? Parents, teachers, school people, why are we not stopping this display of immoral values from the NEA? Parents and teachers, make up a hedge, take a stand, stand in the gap and put a stop to this gross immorality!** My dear friends, parents, and teachers who are paying dues to this organization, listen: *What they call "extremist and radical" is no more than doing what is right. The NEA people should not be in the place of authority to indoctrinate our children with immoral values. They are in effect calling evil good and good evil.* And, that is exactly what the Bible says will happen when a nation forgets God. Isaiah 5:20 says, "Woe unto them that call evil good, and good evil; that put darkness for light, and light for darkness," and in Jeremiah 4:22, "They are wise to do evil, but to do good they have no knowledge."

Friend, do you see by these examples how the NEA attacks Christian values? *Parents and teachers, these are the people you are sending your children to for an education in atheism, evolution, humanism, and the homosexual lifestyle.* Our tax dollars are going to this kind of organization to destroy the minds of our children. Our family values and Christian homes are under attack by the NEA and some public school leaders. Again, much of the efforts of the NEA in time and money go to promote and support the radical socialist agenda, and to attack Christian conservative people and organizations, *with little effort given to improve our public school education.*

The NEA, therefore, does not appear to be in the business of educating our children, but primarily supporting the spread of immorality, and of political left-wing socialist ideology. *Does this alarm you, folks? It should outrage you, especially "now that you know the rest of the story." Think about it, beloved, and while you are doing so, think about this again: The NEA is in the process of trying to make it mandatory, if they have not already done so, for all public schools to include in their curriculum the teaching of homosexuality/lesbian lifestyle. Young boys and girls will be exposed to this outrageous sin using money taken from America's families—our hard earned money is promoting this abominable wickedness.*

And while the NEA is indoctrinating your children into gross sin, they have all but eliminated the true history books of America out of the schools. It seems there is no longer a requirement to read and learn about America's beginning and about our Founding Fathers—America's Christian heritage. *In other words, it appears that the NEA's goal is to erase everything about God out of the school system, and replace God with satanic atheistic teachings. May God have mercy on our nation and forgive our sins!*

Once Satan has infiltrated and has control of our kindergartens through our colleges, and universities, then he controls our society and our nation. You say, "I never knew this was going on," and that is the way they want it—hitting unsuspecting Americans blindsided. For a *complete* discussion of "Grading the NEA" with step-by-step procedures on how to get involved and make your voice count, I **strongly recommend** that parents and teachers obtain a copy of this booklet from Focus on the Family, Colorado Springs, CO 80995-7009. If you care at all about your children's educational future and our nation, I *strongly* suggest that you order more than one and share the booklets along with John Stormer's book *None Dare Call it Education* with your neighbors as well.

The Means by Which Satan Is Destroying America

Dear friend, you need to get involved now. If you do not get involved and be concerned for your children and the future of this nation, then you will lose them and remain in the dark wondering why your children act and think the way they do. Write to your senators and congressmen, even the president, and let them know what is taking place, and **demand** that this kind of NEA leadership be removed and replaced with good conservative people who really care about children and will honor the America family.

As I said at the outset of this message, most Americans do not know what is taking place under their nose, including some of the teachers. The spiritual terrorist forces of Satan are in the process of destroying our nation from within and we are allowing this to take place by not doing a thing about it. **Get involved, parents, and stand in the gap!**

Let us take a closer look at the kind of education we are allowing to be taught to our young children, and that is the indoctrination of the following teaching horses, starting with evolution:

5. Evolution

One of the big reasons why our society and nation is in such a depraved condition is the satanic teaching of evolution in our public school system, colleges, and universities. Satan put the thought of evolution in the mind of a person called Darwin, and that is how it all started. It came from the depraved mind of man, not from God. God is the author of truth. This is Satan's attempt to discredit the creation account in God's Word. And I must say he has done a superb job of lying and deceiving multitudes of Americans, especially the young minds of our children.

I can understand our young children believing a lie, because they trust their parents and believe that they are going to hear the truth in school. God help you parents for sending your innocent babies to false teachers. We who *know* that there is a Supreme Being *know* that He is the Creator of all things, including man. Many of Americans know this to be true as well, and yet we knowingly send our children to these false teachers. Dear parents, I want you to know that your hard-earned dollars are supporting false teachers, and God will hold us responsible. And that is something to think about—seriously!

The true Christian knows without a shadow of doubt that God is real and true. And the reason is because true Christians possess the very presence of the Spirit of God in their hearts. The very life of God is a witness to His creative acts. While the above thoughts may be disturbing your mind at this point, pause with me for a simple question. From where did the names for earth, heaven, day, night, light, darkness, morning, evening, seven days, tree, stars, man, woman, animals, etc come? Names like these we take for granted and do not even give a second thought to how and where they came. Let us find the answer to my question, for you will soon discover where these names came from by recounting the greatest of events in the more recent history of our world and our nation.

Do you remember the monumental historic event on Christmas Eve in 1968, when the American astronauts, Col. Frank Borman, Maj. William A. Anders, and Capt. James A. Lovell Jr. circled the Moon in their spaceship, *Apollo 8?* Over thirty-one years ago, most of the world was listening to this historical space adventure unfold and heard this account when these three American astronauts read these words during their ninth orbit of the moon:

> *"In the beginning God created the heaven and the earth. And the earth was without form and void; and darkness was upon the face of the deep. And the Spirit of God moved upon the face of the waters. And God said, let there be light: and there was light. And God*

The Means by Which Satan Is Destroying America

saw the light, that it was good: and God divided the light from the darkness. And God called the light Day, and the darkness he called Night, And the evening and the morning were the first day. And God said, Let there be a firmament in the midst of the waters, and let it divide the waters from the waters. And God made the firmament and divided the waters which were under the firmament from the waters which were above the firmament; and it was so. And God called the firmament Heaven. And the evening and the morning were the second day. And God said, Let the waters under the heaven be gathered together unto one place, and let the dry land appear: and it was so. And God called the dry land Earth; and the gathering together of the waters called he Seas: and God saw that it was good" (Genesis 1: 1-10).

After Col. Frank Borman, Maj. William A. Anders, and Capt. James A. Lovell Jr. of *Apollo 8* finished reading the first ten verses from the Bible, Gods Word, they said, **"God bless all of you on the good earth."** What a great moment in the history of the world and America, when most of the world heard God's Word and the creation account from outer space for the very first time. No doubt about it, the providence of God brought this event about and allowed Americans to orbit the Moon first with His message to the world.

It was a proper time, for it was Christmas time, when we honor the birth of God's Son, the Lord Jesus Christ, into His world. Yes, Jesus Christ, the sinless One who created all things, and Who came to be like one of His creation in order to die on the cross as a sacrifice for the sins of the world. He then rose from the dead and went back to God His Father in heaven to offer His creation the gift of Salvation and eternal life. "The gift of God is eternal life through Jesus Christ our Lord" (Romans 6:23).

There is a spectacular climax to the astronauts' reading from the first book of the Bible as they circled the Moon: God says in the last book of the Bible, "Behold he [Jesus Christ] cometh with clouds; and every eye shall see him, and they also which pierced him: and all kindreds of the earth shall wail because of him" (Revelation 1:7). Yes, Jesus Christ is coming back to this earth *from outer space,* and "every eye shall see him." Many people thought this would be impossible before the advent of TV and computers. But humanly speaking, we all know now how it may come about very soon. (*However,* God can cause every eye to see Him without the means of electronics.)

Young people, did you find some of the names in the above account? Our young people were not even born at this momentous time in our nation's history when we heard those breathtaking words from the astronauts' space adventure. The young minds of these children who were not born at that time have since been subjected to the false teaching of evolution. And without a doubt, the reading of the creation account by these three astronauts may never be included in any of the schoolbooks. Young people, ask your schoolteachers about this, and see what they say.

Now we know the answer to my question, but just for the record, the following verses are the rest of the six days of the creation account: As we read the above and read the verses below, we can understand that God named His creative acts, even names like "seed," "herb," and "grass," etc.

> *"And God said, let the earth bring forth grass, the herb yielding seed, and the fruit tree yielding fruit after his kind, whose seed is in itself, upon the earth: and it was so. And the earth brought forth grass, and*

The Means by Which Satan Is Destroying America

herb yielding seed after his kind, and the tree yielding fruit whose seed was in itself, after his kind: and God saw that it was good. And the evening and morning were the third day. And God said, Let there be lights in the firmament of the heaven to divide the day from the night; and let them be for signs, and for seasons, and for days, and years: And let them be for lights in the firmament of the heaven to give light upon the earth: and it was so. And God made the two great lights; the greater light to rule the day, and the lesser light to rule the night: he made the stars also. And God set them in the firmament of the heaven to give light upon the earth, And to rule over the day and over the night, and to divide the light from the darkness; and God saw that it was good. And the evening and the morning were the fourth day. And God said, Let the waters bring forth abundantly the moving creature that hath life, and fowl that may fly above the earth in the open firmament of heaven. And God created great whales, and every living creature that moveth, which the waters brought forth abundantly, after their kind, and every winged fowl after his kind, and God saw that it was good. And God blessed them, saying Be fruitful, and multiply, and fill the waters in the seas, and let fowl multiply in the earth. And the evening and the morning were the fifth day. And God said, Let the earth bring forth the living creature after his kind, cattle, and creeping thing and beast of the earth after his kind; and it was so. And God made the beast of the earth after his kind, and cattle after their kind, and every thing that creepeth upon the earth after his kind: and God saw that it was good. And God said, Let us make man after our image, after our likeness: and let them have dominion over the fish of the *sea, and over the fowl of the air, and over the cattle, and over all the earth, and over every creeping thing that creepeth upon the earth. So God created man in his own image, in the image of God created he him; male and female created he them. And God blessed them, and God said unto them, Be fruitful, and multiply, and replenish the earth, and subdue it: and have dominion over the fish of the sea, and over the fowl of the air, and over every living thing that moveth upon the earth. And God said, Behold, I have given you every herb bearing seed, which is upon the face of all the earth, and every tree, in the which is the fruit of a tree yielding seed; to you it shall be for meat. And to every beast of the earth, and to every fowl of the air, and to every thing that creepeth upon the earth, wherein there is life, I have given every green herb for meat: and it was so. And God saw every thing that he made, and, behold, it was very good. And the evening and the morning were the sixth day. Thus the heavens and the earth were finished, and all the host of them. And on the seventh day God ended his work which he had made; and he rested on the seventh day from all his work which he had made" (Genesis 1:11-2:2).*

Every time I read the creation account, it is breathtaking to me, and I have to say, "WOW, how great and awesome is our God!" By the way, God did give to Adam, His creation, the responsibility and incredible *ability* to give names to *all* of God's other creations:

Genesis 2:19-20 "And out of the ground the Lord God formed every beast of the field, and brought them unto Adam to see what he would call them: and whatsoever Adam called every living creature, that was the name thereof. And Adam gave names to all cattle, and to the fowl of the air, and to every beast of the field."

There was one other name given by Adam, and of all names, think about this one:

"And Adam said, This is now bone of my bones, and flesh of my flesh; she shall be called Woman, because she was taken out of Man" (Genesis 2:23).

Now we know where all these names came from, even the names of all the stars:

Psalm 147:4 "He telleth the number of the stars; he calleth them all by their names."

The *point of all this is simply a question: Can the "big bang" of evolution bring all of this into being, along with the names? The answer is absolutely not.* Now, I challenge you to read the rest of the Bible, God's Word, for the greatest adventure of your life, for it will change your thinking and your life forever.

Now, having said all that, I hasten to say, "Satan, the devil, knows God's Word is true, but does not want us, God's creation, to believe it." Did you hear what I just said? Go back and reread that statement until you believe it! In Genesis 3, Satan appeared in the form of a serpent, and visited Eve in the Garden of Eden. And, it was just after God had spoken to Adam and Eve and warned them about a particular tree in the Garden saying,

"Of every tree of the garden thou mayest freely eat: But of the tree of the knowledge of good and evil, thou shalt not eat of it: for in the day that thou eatest thereof thou shalt surely die" (Genesis 2:16-17).

Then Satan said to Eve, "Yea, hath God said…?" Satan is whispering the same kind of thoughts to us today saying, **"There is no God; you were not created; you evolved."** And so, the devil has recruited his many teachers and professors to teach us that we were not a product of creation, but of evolution. And he has deceived millions of Americans and especially our young people around the world into believing this lie. Satan is the father of lies in John 8:44. Satan appears to make things sound right—"Satan himself is transformed into an angel of light" (2 Corinthians 11:14). Satan appears to us as one who speaks the truth. Dear friend, if we never read God's Book, then we **live in spiritual darkness, believing Satan's lies:** We will never **know the truth, that God is the author of absolute truth.**

Those who do not accept God do not accept the truth— they live a lie. And so, we have many so-called scholars and professors in universities, colleges and public school teachers who are so willing and foolish as to believe the devil's lies!

Not too long ago I had an occasion to go to Huntsville, Alabama, and while there I visited the space center. I picked up a little booklet in which a question was asked about everything we see: "How did all of this come into being?" The answer was, "A big bang happened and brought this universe into being." I thought to myself, "Oh, my soul, we have these so-called 'scholarly scientists' *whom God enabled to create a huge spaceship out of His creative elements.* These astronauts travel to God's created Moon and back, orbit His created Earth, and then these 'scholarly scientists' write the most laughable and stupid statement that I have ever heard—it just blows my mind!" This has got to be depravity and stupidity at the highest level! This is so incredibly tragic because man has chosen to believe the lies of Satan rather then God's *truth*.

Dear friend, the lie of evolution is an insult to our God-given intelligence. Satan is having a field day laughing at us for believing his lies and remaining in spiritual darkness of unbelief. Satan is truly making "fools" out of us! Again I say, "*Incredible!*"

God says in His Word, "Professing themselves to be wise, they became fools" (Romans 1:22); "Ever learning, and never able to come to the knowledge of the truth" (2 Timothy 3:7). I say again, "It really does not take much *to deceive people with lies. It is really easy to believe a lie rather than the truth.*"

Again, God's Word says, "God is not a man, that he should lie" (Numbers 23:19); "*Let God be true and every man a liar*" (Romans 3:4); "God that cannot lie" (Titus 1:2), and it is "impossible for God to lie" (Hebrews 6:18). *It is these teachers, professors, and scientist that have* "changed the truth of God into a lie" (Romans 1:25).

Thank the Lord for those astronauts who knew the truth. I play the tape of that breathtaking space event every now and then. Yes, Satan is laughing at our stupidity. We willingly accept lies, but not the truth.

Evolution exists only in the darkened mind of man. *It is a proven fact that evolution cannot be proven as a scientific fact.* The "learned" evolutionists are still trying desperately to dig up evidence to prove their theory, but it will never happen folks, because evolution never happened. These lies of evolution are being taught to the young eager and innocent minds of our children in the public schools *as truth*. By the time they enter high school, they accept it as a fact without question. We Americans have allowed this false teaching to dominate our public school system, as well as our colleges and universities. My question is simply this: WHY? *Why have we allowed this foolish lie to be taught to our children?* One of the reasons is because of what I said at the outset of this message; We *simply do not want to get involved*. And besides, a large number of us send our children to Christian schools where they are not exposed to the lie of evolution. Well, this is good, and I wish every child could go to a Christian school, *but that is not happening*. As a result, the lie of evolution is dangerously impacting our society and nation, dear friend.

We are on the verge of losing our nation to these horses—terrorists of Satan. I venture to guess that most Americans do not even care about the public schools indoctrination of lies into the minds of their children. *Young people and parents, how would you feel if someone lied to you continually? If you are normal, you would not stay around that kind of person very long, or would you? I ask you this question: Do you want your teachers and professors to continue to teach the lie of evolution to you? Young people and parents,* **it is time to take a stand** *against school leaders and teachers who are using your hard-earned money to lie to you and your children!* **Take a stand** *and strongly suggest that they stop teaching lies and start teaching the truth about Creation from the Bible, the Book of Truth! May God help you to do it!* God says in Revelation 21:8, "All liars shall have their part in the lake of fire." Think about that, teachers and professors! Read section 8 below in conjunction with the above.

Let us look at another "educational" satanic horse that has and is destroying the minds of our young people and adults:

6. *Humanism*

Evolution breeds humanism. If we were not created, and there is no God, then we are our own gods. We are able to do everything ourselves; we do not need a God to tell us what to do or not to do. We can decide that for ourselves; this is what Adam and Eve thought. We can accomplish anything and everything on our own; look at all we have accomplished thus far; we invented the technology that we are enjoying and so who needs God; we can do everything ourselves if we set our minds to it. Sound familiar? Well, humanly speaking, it seems that we have come a long way in advancement of "our knowhow" and of "our capabilities."

This is basically what humanism is about—the worship of man and what man has accomplished. But I say, *"WHOA to this deceiving horse!"* Jesus Christ, the Son of the true and living God, says this, "Without me you can do nothing" (John 15:5). Listen carefully, dear friend. *Jesus Christ created you and gave you a heart that beats and breath to breathe, so you can live to accomplish what God has enabled you to do.*

Have you ever thought about what causes your heart to beat without gas or diesel fuel? Is it you that keeps that pump in you, called the heart, beating and pumping blood throughout your body day and night, without stopping, all the years of your life? No, my friend, only God our Creator can do something like that.

My daddy lived to reach ninety-nine years before his heart stopped beating. A man-made mechanical pump will fail after a few years and need to be replaced. It will not last for 100 years. What we think we have done on our own is what God has enabled us to accomplish. So, without Jesus Christ, we can do nothing on our own. We did nothing to create ourselves, and we certainly cannot keep our hearts beating and ourselves breathing without the sustaining work and power of God. It is God our great Creator who put within the mind He created the ability to discover and to create something from something created. *But, it is God who created something out of nothing.* Think about that, friend!

Humanistic philosophy is being taught to our children in our public schools, and to our young people in our colleges and universities, including our businesses. No wonder our young people are coming out of our school system unaware of an existing and living God. And, we are allowing this to continue in our schools without any opposition. WHY?

Apparently, we do not have it in us to understand what is going on around us.

Most Americans live as if there were no God; they become willingly blinded to what is devouring and destroying our nation of young people. As a result, when America heard the song "God Bless America" being sung, no doubt for the first time ever in public by our congressmen and senators, many of our children never knew the song existed. We have been hiding God from them all these years and letting them sit under teachers of darkness who worship the false god of humanism.

It is a tragedy that it takes a tragedy to humble Americans before Almighty God in order to call upon Him! May God have mercy on our nation! By the way, there are other songs besides "God Bless America" that honor God and two of them are "My Country tis of Thee" and "America the Beautiful." Ask your children if they have heard these songs? You will find these songs in the church hymnal, but rarely sung except on patriotic days, if then. And if your children never go to church, they will never hear these great songs honoring God. Instead they will hear the lies of Satan's workers indoctrinating them with their teaching of *evolution and humanism*. No wonder we are experiencing a moral collapse of our society, with sin reigning and devouring our young people.

Again, we should not have been singing "God Bless America" at that time, because that was an insult to God. You see, God has been blessing America all these years and given us this freedom to enjoy. But, America has not recognized that it is God who sustains us, supplies all our needs, feeds us, enables us with abilities to live and work together as families and as a society. It is God who has poured out His blessings on our nation and has kept our homeland from being attacked and destroyed by barbaric nations until now. Because of God, America won the war over Germany and

Japan. *Our cry to God who has blessed our nation should be, "God have mercy on us and forgive our sins."* And one of our sins is humanism. This is what our God is waiting and wanting to hear from America. May God help us to confess our sins, rise up and take a stand against the sin of humanism!

Parents, it is incredible that we would allow our children to be taught lies day after day, and not speak out against this evil. Would you habitually lie to your children day after day? I think not. Then rise up par*ents of America, stand in the gap against the NEA, against the teaching of atheism, evolution and humanism! Let us remove from our schools, colleges and universities these satanic doctrines, and install teachers who will encourage our young people in the truth!*

Let us look together at another gigantic horse that is greatly impacting our nation and our public school system, the ACLU:

7. The ACLU

As a nation, we have not been giving God the praise and honor due Him. For years, we have been told not to mention the name of our God in our public school system, or in government, by an organization that is called the ACLU. The ACLU stands for American Civil Liberties Union. The ACLU and other sister organizations such as People for the American Way and Americans United for the Separation of Church and State are determined to eliminate God not only from government, public places, and schools, but from America.

In the beginning, the ACLU organization seemingly started in the right direction, but over the years went to the left of their agenda and used their "liberty" to grossly misinterpret the First Amendment to the Constitution. The First Amendment plainly states, "Congress shall make no law respecting an establishment of religion, or prohibiting the free exercise thereof; or abridging the freedom of speech, or of the press; or the right of the people peaceably to assemble, and to petition the government for a redress of grievances."

The first part of the amendment is what the ACLU believes to have the only and right interpretation. Read the first part again: "Congress shall make no law respecting an establishment of religion, or prohibiting the free exercise thereof." What does this plainly say? I think that any school-age person can give us the proper meaning of this statement. This is what it says: Congress shall not make a law respecting, favoring, or endorsing one particular religion to be the official state religion, and shall not make a law against the freedom to establish and practice religion. In other words, there can be many religions established in America and freely practiced, but not a national religion. Our Founding Fathers inserted this amendment to the Constitution because England had a state religion—The Church of England. This is the reason why America is here and not part of England; we have freedom to worship according to the religion of our choice, without persecution from state religious leaders.

America does not have a "Church of America." The ACLU wants us to believe that the First Amendment means that there must be a separation of religion (ACLU uses the term "Church") from the state and federal government and from state and federal supported agencies. They say that every time an individual or groups of individuals use government subsidized public facilities such as schools, colleges, universities, and other public places to pray and carry a Bible, or to read the Bible, or mention the name of God, and to display the Ten Commandments that the government is endorsing, favoring, or establishing a certain religion called Christianity. Really! Is that what the First Amendment means? Absolutely NOT!

To mention the name of God or to pray is not establishing a religion. The First Amendment *does not say* that you cannot do any of the activities mentioned above, including saying the Pledge of Allegiance in public schools. The writers of the Constitution did not have any such thing in mind. In fact, in early America, prayer and worship services were held in government facilities. Read the history of early America. Just to mention God in school and government, or recite the Pledge of Allegiance to the American flag is not establishing a religion, but simply *patriotism, and recognizing that God our Creator is very much in control of the affairs of our nation.*

Let us set the record straight; Christianity is not a religion, but a *spiritual relationship with Jesus Christ, the Son of God,* "Christ in you" (Colossians 1:27). There are many religions, but only one true relationship. The ACLU has set out to get the American public to swallow their phony interpretation, and has succeeded in doing this very thing. However, I say this in all sincerity and love—I believe sometimes individuals as well as organizations believe they are sincerely ministering a service of good will to this nation; but in fact their minds are blinded by the god of this world system—Satan. This they do without realizing it, as the Bible says, "The god of this world hath blinded the minds of them which believe not" (2 Corinthians 4:4).

And so, the ACLU folks are having our nation believing their lies. *And once more, they have set themselves up as having the official accepted interpretation of the First Amendment! I ask, "Who gave them that right?"* What is so unbelievable is that the American population, as well as a major part of the Christian community, has allowed this false teaching to continue all these years. Therefore, the ACLU has become a god to multitudes of Americans. Satan can cause people to believe the most unbelievable and foolish lies.

My dear America friends do not be deceived. Take a stand for God and country! Fear God, rather than man! Let us put the ACLU and other like organizations out of business once and for all; otherwise, our beloved nation will become entirely heathen like other godless nations. The ACLU is apparently trying to destroy our liberty and freedom—the very thing that allows them to say what they say. *To honor God is not establishing a religion.* Again, it was God who gave birth to this nation so we could have freedom of speech and religion. We should obey our God and not the ACLU god. Our God says, "Blessed is the nation whose God is the Lord" (Psalm 33:12). Again, this is why we honor God, and have **"In God We Trust"** on our currency and coins, and have **"One nation under God"** in our pledge of allegiance.

Bear with me in my overwhelming desire to praise and worship our God for giving to us this great nation. I want to share with you again why we honor God, by listening to *the words* of the songs of America. **"God Bless America"**

> "God Bless America, land that I love,
> stand beside her and guide her
> thru the night with the light from above,
> from the mountains to the prairie
> to the ocean white with foam,
> God bless America, my home sweet home,
> God bless America, my home sweet home."

Again, **"My Country Tis Of Thee"**

> "My country tis of Thee,
> sweet land of liberty, of Thee I sing:
> Land where my fathers died,
> land of the pilgrim's pride,
> from every mountain side
> let freedom ring."

The Means by Which Satan Is Destroying America

And the last verse,

"Our fathers' God to Thee,
Author of liberty, of Thee we sing:
long may our land be bright with freedom's holy light;
protect us by thy might, Great God our King."

And, one verse from the song *"America the Beautiful,"*

"O beautiful for spacious skies,
for amber waves of grain,
for purple mountain majesties above the fruited plain,
America! America!
God shed His grace on thee,
and crown thy good with brotherhood, from sea to shining sea."

In New York harbor stands a beautiful lady, the **Statue of Liberty**, for all the world to see and to read these beautiful inscribed words:

"Give me your tired, your poor.
Your huddled masses yearning to breath free,
The wretched refuse of your teeming shore.
Send these, the homeless, tempest-tossed to me:
I lift my lamp beside the golden door!"

Jesus said in Matthew 11:28, "Come unto me, all ye that labor and are heavy laden, and I will give you rest."

Let us include a song that many Americans have never heard called **"Statue of Liberty"**[13] with beautiful music, and these glorifying words:

> "In New York harbor stands a lady, with a torch raised to the sky.
> And all who see her know she stands for liberty for you and me.
> I'm so proud to be called an American, to be named with the brave and the free.
> I will honor our flag, and our trust in God, and the Statue of Liberty.
> On lonely Golgotha stood a cross with my Lord raised to the sky.
> And all who kneel there live forever, as all the saved can testify.
> I'm so glad to be called a Christian, to be named with the ransomed and whole,
> As the Statue liberates the citizen, so the cross liberates the soul.
> Oh, the cross is my Statue of Liberty, it was there that my soul was set free.
> Unashamed I'll proclaim that a rugged cross is my Statue of Liberty, my liberty."

And, then there is the song, *"God of Our Fathers, Whose Almighty hand"* with these words:

> "Thy love divine hath led us in the past,
> in this free land by thee our lot is cast;
> Be thou our ruler, guardian, guide and stay,
> thy word our law, thy paths our chosen way."

Other songs like *"Battle Hymn of the Republic"* with the words of the last verse,

> "In the beauty of the lilies Christ was born across the sea,
> with a glory in His bosom that transfigures you and me;

as He died to make men holy, let us live to make men free; while God is marching on."

And finally, America's national anthem *"The Star-Spangled Banner"*—the last verse which is rarely ever sung says,

"Oh, thus be it ever, when men shall stand between their
   loved homes and the war's desolation;
Blest with victory and peace, may the Heav'n rescued land
   Praise the Power that hath made and preserved us a
   nation!
Then conquer we must, when our cause it is just; and this
   be our motto:
'In God is our trust!' And the star-spangled banner in tri-
   umph shall wave O'er the land of the free, and the
   home of the brave."

Dear friend, I ask you these questions: How did these great songs with these powerful words transpire? How did these words get on our currency and coins and in our pledge of allegiance to our flag? And how did the name of God appear, or is implied on the Declaration of Independence and Constitution, and all over our nation's capital and monuments in and around Washington, DC?

I will tell you how: In the first place, no person could have penned the words and music to those songs except under inspiration from God. Secondly, godly *men and women in early America recognized that it was under the providence of God our Creator, and only by God's grace and mercy, that He raised up this nation out of nothing to demonstrate to the rest of the world what happens when people and a nation honor the true God.*

But I hasten to say, "Many Americans are tragically unaware or willingly blinded to what I have said thus far in this book."

And for many of our young people, this is the first time they have ever seen the words to these songs. As for my dear ACLU friends and others like you, I have a short message for you: *This was God's nation before you came on the scene, and America will still be God's nation when you pass off the scene.*

America, we are allowing our God-given freedoms to be taken away by these organizations. We are allowing sin, corruption and the lies of Satan to control and corrupt our minds. Take away God, and we take away freedom and our nation. My friend, at this very time when we are seeing "God Bless America," and "In God We Trust" being displayed all across this great land of God, and especially during the Christmas season, the ACLU and many of our public school leadership are taking everything that portrays Christmas and the true meaning of Christmas out of the public schools. And it is all because of this god, the ACLU, that has raised itself up to deceive Americans. America is **bowing down in obedience and worship** to the ACLU when we should be bowing down to Jehovah God, the true God of America. It would be almost laughable if it were not so TRAGIC! Satan is having a field day laughing at the Christians in God's nation. *We do not have to obey or yield to the ACLU!*

More recently, in one or two public schools in California, and in one or two universities, an Eastern religion that worships a false god is being taught, and the ACLU is not doing any thing about it. Why is the ACLU not protesting this outrage? The answer is found in Matthew 12:26, "If Satan cast out Satan, he is divided against himself; how shall then his kingdom stand?" In other words, Satan is not against his systems of destruction. He rejoices at this victory! **Wake up America, and take a stand before it is too late. Join forces and stand against the ACLU and your public schools; strongly suggest that Christmas and our God be put back into the** schools as well as all the documents that made this nation great. America's voice must be heard! Do not allow a handful of legally blinded minds to deceive us and run over us with their lies. The ACLU is *not* the voice of the majority of Americans.

Wake up and stand in the gap, make up a hedge of righteousness throughout this nation, and run with the terrorists and let them know the true God of this nation! We do not need these destroyers to tell us what we can and cannot do. If the ACLU workers do not like the greatest nation on the face of this planet, and America's God-given freedom, then I say to you dear friends, "You are *free* to go elsewhere—to godless nations and enjoy tyranny instead of freedom!" Maybe then they will realize the beauty and preciousness of true freedom.

Dear friend, open your spiritual eyes and do not allow anti-God, anti-Christ, anti-Christian, and anti-freedom haters to use our freedom that they enjoy, and with this freedom destroy our beloved America. Wake up and rise up, America! Look around at our nation being destroyed within by the ACLU. Make up a hedge, stand in the gap, run with these footmen and horses armed with the Word of God!

I have discussed a number of major horses that are destroying this nation, but I want to mention another gigantic horse, and *this horse is the cause of all the other destructive horses.* There is a principle called "cause and effect." Where there is an effect, there is a cause for it. I believe all of these horses are the effects of one cause, and that cause is *atheism.*

8. Atheism

What is atheism? Simply stated, the belief that there is no God. But God says in His Word, the Bible, "The fool hath said in his heart, no God" (Psalm 14:1). God calls an atheist a fool. In Romans 1:19-20 God says,

"Because that which may be known of God is manifest in them: for God hath shewed it unto them. For the invisible things of him from the creation of the world are clearly seen, being understood by the things that are made, even his eternal power and Godhead; so that they are without excuse."

Dear friend, it does not matter if we deny God, for He has put within our being the ability to understand that He does exist! And one day the atheists will stand before our Creator and be judged for their unbelief. My definition of an atheist is one who wishes that there were no God. God says in His Word, **"Come now let us reason together"** (Isaiah 1:18). Let us *think* about this as I return to the evolution horse to illustrate a point. But, actually there is no difference between the two—atheism breeds evolution.

The atheist/evolutionist would have us believe that everything came about by a big bang, and humans evolved from the ape. I ask the question: How can a big bang *without intelligence* bring into existence a universe of order, and *intelligence*? How can a human race with *intelligence* evolve out of animal life without intelligence? Will the atheist *with the intelligence of a monkey* explain that to me! *Dear friend, it is impossible!* Plain old common sense will tell us that *it takes a superior intelligent being to create a race of people with intelligence.* But common sense is lacking in most of our public school systems and "schools of higher learning."

While you are *thinking* about that, *think* about this: As we look up in the night sky, we see a breathtaking scene: "thousand billion stars in the sky…that generate their own power to keep them on course…the earth spins at a given speed without slowing up so that we have day and night…tilts so that we get our seasons…The inexhaustible envelope of air, only 50 miles deep, and of exactly the right density to support human life ...The sun stokes a fire just warm enough to sustain us on earth, but not hot enough to fry us or cold enough to kill us"[14] somehow just "banged" itself into existence—*impossible*. The psalmist David said in Psalm 19:1, "The heavens declare the glory of God; and the firmament sheweth his handywork."

Again, let us *think* about our human body: as we stand back in awe, we understand that the human "body contains about 2,500,000 pores, about 3,000 to the square inch. The human skeleton has more than 200 bones. There are more than 500 muscles, and an equal number of nerves and blood vessels.... Then there is the heart, an unbelievable, rugged organ, a four valve pump which handles 5,000 gallons of blood a day, almost enough to fill a railroad tank car."[15] God says in Leviticus 17:11, "For the life of the flesh is in the blood." The heart "supplies a circulatory system with 12,000 miles of vessels and in the course of a lifetime, beats two and one half billion times. All the blood in our heart is pumped through our heart every minute and the heart beats about 70 times in that time or 100,800 times a day. And consider the sugar thermostat below the human pancreas. It maintains a level of sugar in the human blood sufficient for energy but without it, all of us would fall into a coma and die. The kidneys are among the most intricate organs in the body. They contain approximately 280 miles of tiny tubules whose function is to filter impurities from the blood. In the course of the day, they filter something like 185 quarts of water from the blood, purify it, and return it to the circulation. Normally the adult body contains approximately 24 trillion red cells, which carry oxygen to nourish tissues. Laid edge to edge they would reach half way to the moon."[16]

In a recent discovery in "Micro-Biology" on the human cell, it was reported that the human cell contains machines with a lot of parts in that some are like a motorboat with a propeller that moves the cell through the blood stream.[17] This is an incredible discovery. And then there is "the human mind. It is greater in capacity than a computer the size of the Empire State Building."[18] This body of ours is an incredible creation of a human machine factory of intelligence with the ability to know our Creator. Again, the atheist/evolutionist would have us to believe that chance brought all of this into existence—*impossible*. The psalmist David said to our Great Intelligent Designer—God, "I will praise thee for I am fearfully and wonderfully made, marvelous are thy works, and that my soul knoweth right well" (Psalm 139:14).

My friend, no "big bang" and evolution could ever bring all of this, including monkeys and you, into existence. *It was the work of a superior intelligent Being—God.* Mr. Atheist, what do you think about the wind? Would you say that you do not believe there is such a thing as wind! I do not think you would deny this truth. So I ask you, why since you cannot see it? You say, "Well, *I can feel the effects* of the wind on my face, *see the movement* of the leaves on the trees, and sometimes hear the sound of the wind." The story is told of a teacher asking one of her little students if she could see God. The little girl said, "No." The teacher replied, "Then, there must not be a God!" The little girl thought for a moment and asked her teacher if she could see her brain. The teacher said, "Of course not." The little girl replied, "Then you must not have a brain!" I like that!

Now, I invite you to open your eyes, look all around you, look carefully at yourself, and see the creative effects and beauty of your invisible God. Every created person has a spirit within the body. We cannot see our spirit, but just the same, our spirit resides in this created "house" that God provided for us. When the spirit departs the body, the body is dead (James 2:26). We are as much spiritual beings, and more so, as we are physical beings. This is why we are responsible to our Creator regardless of what we believe, or choose not to believe. The Bible says, "God is a Spirit, and they that worship him must worship *in spirit* and in truth" (John 4:24). Think about all that again, friend, for it should cause us to fall on our face with fear and praise before our awesome Creator.

Listen to another great spiritual truth: The only way a person can enter heaven is to be recreated in Christ Jesus, the Son of God. You see, in the beginning the whole human race was created in Adam, and was given a physical birth into this physical world. But, the physical cannot enter heaven—only the spiritual. We must therefore be spiritually born into the "last Adam," Jesus Christ, or else our destination is hell instead of heaven. This spiritual process is described by Jesus in John 3:1-21 as a process called the "born again" relationship with Jesus Christ. It is not a physical birth but a spiritual birth, as Jesus likens it to the action of the wind, when He said in John 3:8, "The wind bloweth where it listeth, and thou hearest the sound thereof, but canst not tell whence it cometh and whither it goeth: so is every one that is born of the Spirit." Spirit is capitalized here because it is God's Spirit that brings this miracle birth about.

The spirit of atheism in America has produced, or "birthed" evolution, humanism, fornication and adultery; pornography, abortion, murder, homosexuals and lesbians, the ACLU, and other so called legal organizations that have the same agenda as the ACLU. I could go on and on and also mention that socialism and communism are very much alive in America under the guise of liberalism, but the cause of all these effects is atheism or *unbelief.*

The atheist reasons that since there is no God, then obviously the universe must have "banged itself into existence." And because we are the product of evolution, we must be in charge of our own destiny. Look at all we have accomplished on our own—thus *humanism*. Because there is no God, then there is no right or wrong. We can do whatever we please because there are no rules or laws to follow. Thus, we practice the sins of the flesh: *adultery, fornication, pornography, children having children, abortion, sodomy, murder, the teaching of the lies of atheism, evolution and humanism, etc., without retribution, without accountability, so one thinks.*

No wonder there are so many people on *drugs and alcohol committing suicide. Is it therefore any wonder that we have children terrorizing our public schools, shooting and murdering one another!* And it is all because they think they have no reason to live. If there is no God, no life after death, no nothing, then life has no meaning and purpose; therefore, to many of them suicide is a relief, an escape from nothing! This is what these young people call "freedom!" I call it a swamp of quicksand confusion.

But, I want you to know, dear friend, that **life has meaning and a purpose, and it is found in the Lord Jesus Christ. Death is not the end, but the beginning of conscious existence in eternity, either in heaven or hell.** It is your choice! The atheistic, darkened and unbelieving mind does not change the truth of God. If one chooses to stay in unbelief and do nothing, then when you close your eyes for the last time in death, you will no longer be an unbeliever—you will know there is a God, and stand before the God who created you. If this should come true for you, then your time will have come and gone, and it will be too late to do anything about it. What a great tragedy and awakening there is going to be the moment the eyes are closed for the last time on earth!

Where are you going to spend eternity? This is the question every person **must** *answer.* It is up to you. You make the choice while you are physically alive. God our Creator and Sustainer loves you, my friend. I strongly beg of you to get a Bible, God's book of instructions for His creation, read it, embrace it, and surrender your heart to Christ now. "Now is the accepted time; behold, now is the day of salvation" (2 Corinthians 6:2). *What a terrible tragedy to live your allotted physical life without God within your body, and then to die without God and be consciously tormented in the lake of fire for all eternity with that thought.*

Dear friend, do you not see now the gigantic impact atheism has on our nation—its ripple effect? If we allow these evil horses to take God out of our nation, then we die, destroying ourselves, calling it "freedom." The wicked will do what they want and say what they want, and who is to stop them—*this is almost our American way of life today!* Folks, t*his is of Satan.* Satan wants America to be just another atheistic heathen nation as his trophy. And this is the real reason why some of these horses are out to eliminate the name and the mentioning of God from all public places.

America has been deceived all these years into believing the twisted interpretation of the First Amendment. No doubt these horses are *unaware* that they are being used of Satan for this purpose. *Atheism is a god to them—a religion and the worship of atheism.* **But, God** *created the human race to worship Him and have fellowship with Him.* Which way is it going to be, dear friend? *We are fools to allow the spread of atheism and its effects to continue in our nation, a nation that started with God.*

One of the reasons why the spirit of atheism has such an impact on America is because of one gigantic horse that has changed our thinking and devoured our nation's morals and spirituality. This horse is apostasy among the churches and the people.

9. *Apostasy and the Horses Without*

Apostasy is defined as those who have outwardly at one time professed belief in the fundamentals of the Christian faith, (such as, the deity of Jesus Christ, the virgin birth of

Jesus Christ the Son of God, His vicarious death, His shed blood on the cross for our sins, His resurrection from the dead, His ascension to the right hand of the God the Father, and the coming again of Jesus Christ). But they have departed from these essential doctrines of the faith, including salvation through faith in Jesus Christ, and yet still maintain an outward profession of Christianity.

The Bible says,

> *"Now the Spirit speaketh expressly, that in the latter times some shall depart from the faith giving heed to seducing spirits, and doctrines of devils;...Having a form of godliness, but denying the power thereof: ...For the time will come when they will not endure sound doctrine; but after their own lusts shall they heap to themselves teachers, having itching ears; And they shall turn away their ears from the truth, and shall be turned unto fables" (1 Timothy 4:1, 2 Timothy 3:5; 4:3-4).*

I hear the voice of apostasy calling America away from the God of our Founding Fathers, and the God of Israel to other gods and false religions. America, take heed and listen to the admonition from God to his people Israel spoken through Joshua, his servant just before his death:

> *"Be ye therefore very courageous to keep and to do all that is written in the book of the law of Moses, that ye turn not aside there from to the right hand or to the left; That ye come not among these nations, these that remain among you; neither make mention of the name of their gods, nor cause to swear by them, neither serve them, nor bow yourselves unto them; But cleave unto the Lord your God, as ye have done unto*

> this day.... Take good heed therefore unto yourselves that ye love the Lord God.... When ye have transgressed the covenant of the Lord your God, which he commanded you, and have gone and served other gods, and bowed yourself to them; then shall the anger of the Lord be kindled against you, and ye shall perish quickly from off the good land which he hath given unto you" (Joshua 23:6-8,11,16).

Israel turned from their true God to the false idol gods of the surrounding nations. God is saying the same thing to America. And if you will read the next book, Judges, you will see how Israel went into apostasy time after time, and God dealt with them. How tragic that they never learned the joy of obeying God. America is marching to the same beat in the same direction that Israel took that ended in her destruction.

Apostasy is an open door to invite in religious horses. Like Israel's apostasy, our young generation of Americans have grown up without the knowledge of the Christian faith, and along with our older generation are not only departing from the faith, but are embracing the abominable sins of this world's system. Instead of raising our children in Bible-believing churches, we are raising them up on Sunday morning to bow down to the god of TV; during the week, we send them to school where they receive indoctrination in atheism and false religions. As a result, we are witnessing the beginning of embracing the false gods of the Eastern religions all the way up to the leadership of our nation.

Our nation seemly is heading toward being a "multicultural nation." We have for centuries allowed the teaching of false religions, or cults, within our nation. More recently, we have been invaded with Eastern religions—one in particular, about which someone made this statement: "We worship the same God." If this is a true statement, then how come, at the same time that statement was said, the *Bible, The Word of the True and Living God has been cast out of our schools and higher institutions of learning, and being replaced with Eastern religious indoctrination?* This does not sound like the same God!

With all due respect, dear friend, to which god are we bowing? The God I serve, Jehovah God of the Bible, makes us one in Christ Jesus, and we speak the same language. Satan knows truth from error, and that is why the ACLU is not going to do anything about removing the teaching of the Eastern religions out of our schools. This situation must be reversed, friend. We who know the truth are going to have to wake up, make up the hedge for truth and righteousness, and stand in the gap—insisting that this indoctrination of false gods cease immediately, and be removed from our schools, and our nation! **"Learn not the ways of the heathen"** (Jeremiah 10:2).

Multiculturalism was not the intent of our Founding Fathers. In the beginning of our great nation, when our Founding Fathers declared freedom to practice religion, I am convinced that they had in mind the various religious denominations within our nation that worship the God of the Bible. They did not mean to do away with our borders and allow the world to come in at will to include all their false gods from across the ocean. They did not foresee what our nation is experiencing—the invasion of criminals and the religious horses of the world with their false gods. They did not have in mind giving immigrants the "freedom" to worship their gods, to invest millions of dollars in big business, and to spread their teachings in our schools—thus gaining control of America.

Multiculturalism is changing our way of life and religion to the Eastern ways and religion, thus bringing America down to the poverty level of the nations they left. We as a nation in our ignorance and blindness are allowing these foreign nations to take advantage of our so-called religious freedom in order to secure a beachhead in our country. If these people truly came to America to escape their poverty and slavery and to become citizens of our nation, then they need to leave their religions and their gods behind, and honor our God and our way of living.

The reason why they live in poverty is because of their religion. By and large, most of these cultures do not realize the cause of their condition. I personally do not blame them for leaving their poverty and lack of freedom. But to bring with them their religion—the very thing that caused them to leave their country; and then to spread their false teaching in our schools and universities should not be tolerated.

There is the true story in the Bible of two women, a Jewish woman whose name was Naomi, and Ruth from the country of Moab. Naomi went with her husband and two sons to Moab because of the famine in Judah. After living for some time in Moab, Naomi's husband died along with her two sons, leaving Naomi and her daughters-in-law. Naomi decided to go back to her people, and she wanted both daughters-in-law to return to Moab. One returned to her people and her gods, but the other one, Ruth, embraced and pleaded with Naomi to take her back with her. Listen to the words of Ruth from the book of Ruth 1:14-16, verse 16:

> "And Ruth said, Intreat me not to leave thee, or to return from following after thee: for whither thou goest, I will go; and where thou lodgest, I will lodge; thy people shall be my people, and thy God my God."

If these cultures truly *desire only* to become citizens of America, then they must be willing to *abide by our Constitution, pledge allegiance to the flag of the United States of*

America, honor our God, and our way of life, including our English language. If they are not willing to commit themselves, then I say this in love, "They can go back with their religion from where they came, lest our nation be destroyed by their religion and brought down to the poverty level of their countries they left." This is only fair, dear friend!

If this situation is not reversed, then we as a nation in ignorance will follow our top religious and national leadership into complete apostasy. Again, listen carefully to the warnings from God to the churches and our nation:

> *"But there were false prophets also among the people, even as there shall be false teachers among you, who privily shall bring in damnable heresies, even denying the Lord that bought them and bring upon themselves swift destruction. And many shall follow their pernicious ways; by reason of whom the way of truth shall be evil spoken of" (2 Peter 2:1-2).*

Again it says, "**the way of truth shall be evil spoken of.**" Not too long ago, a prominent senator spoke evil of a university that stands up for the truth and the fundamentals of the Christian faith. This was during an approval session of a candidate for attorney general of the United States. I believe a large number of our politicians as well as our church denominations of this nation have and are turning away from the truth—denying the doctrines of the faith, and that Jesus Christ is the only way to God's heaven.

Our nation is departing from the truth. Jesus said, "**I am the way, the truth, and the life, no man cometh unto the Father, but by me**" (John 14:6). Because Jesus Christ, the only begotten Son of God, died as the sacrificial Lamb of God for *all the sins of the world,* then He truly is the only way to heaven and to the Father for all people. The Bible says,

> "Neither is there salvation in any other; for there is none other name under heaven given among men, whereby we must be saved" (Acts 4:12).
>
> "Behold the Lamb of God, which taketh away the sin of the world" (John 1:29).
>
> "For God so loved the world that he gave his only begotten son that whosoever beliveth on him should not perish but have everlasting life" (John 3:16).
>
> "The Father sent the Son to be the Saviour of the world" (1 John 4:14).
>
> "That the world may believe" (John 17:21).

If the religions of this world deny these great truths, they are false religions and false gods.

My friend, apostasy and our other sins are devouring the moral and spiritual foundation of our great nation. Is it any wonder that Satan has let loose all these horses upon our nation and is in the process of infiltrating our nation with his religious horses that were once outside our nation? *America must stop the influx of Eastern religions and return to faith in Jesus Christ before we continue to destroy ourselves. We must turn from our wicked ways and come back to the true and living God of the Bible.*

One of God's graces is that of longsuffering, or patience, not willing that any should perish. But how long do we think God will stand idly by and not react to all our wickedness and corruption? On September 11, 2001, the Twin Towers in New York, came tumbling down, and part of the Pentagon was destroyed. Nearly three thousand Americans were murdered and went out into eternity, either to heaven or hell. It was like a warning shot across the bow of a ship. We need to wake up, America! The radical terrorist horses are already within, and are coming! "If thou hast run with the footmen, and they have wearied thee, then how canst thou contend with the horses? And if in the land of peace, wherein thou trustedst, they wearied thee, then how wilt thou do in the swelling of Jordan?" *Are we not sensing the swelling of evil within and without our nation?* **Can we not see our world and our nation rushing toward the prophetic end time—the beginning of the end?**

At the outset of this message, I alluded to nations without, who are using our technology to build up their armed forces with our so-called trade agreements; these nations are just waiting in the wings, biding their time until they come against us. While they are waiting, the terrorist horses within our nation are destroying us morally and spiritually; meanwhile, we are chasing terrorist around the world, thus weakening us militarily. Then, when the terrorist nations without believe they can destroy or finish us off, they will come. **Make no mistake about it, friend; they will come!**

America is a coveted prize for some nations. For example, I wonder how many Americans are aware that Russia and China have the capability of reaching America with missiles! Furthermore, while America is **"in bed with Communist China"** and calling it "a trade agreement," China controls the Panama Canal! Folks, the next time you go shopping at the larger department stores, before you purchase the items, check out the labels and see where they are made! **The ones that take America down win the world.** It is time to wake up, America and listen! Psalm 9:17 says, *"The wicked shall be turned into hell, and all nations that forget God."* Let us not allow our great land so rich in freedom, wealth, and opportunities be destroyed through ignorance by being uninformed. Our nation is a precious gift from our God; let us do all that we can to protect this precious gift.

The Means by Which Satan Is Destroying America

Allow me now as I said I would do at the beginning of this book to share my heart with you who make up America. During July 2001, I was traveling and turned on the motel T.V. to watch the news. I went to bed saddened and mentally weary by what I had seen. I watched homosexuals and lesbians engaged in kissing their kind and dancing in a public place as if it were the normal thing to do, while newsmen were interviewing some activists about their so-called rights as Americans. During the middle of the night, I was suddenly awakened, and I began to cry about the tragedy that had unfolded on the news channel just before I turned it off. I found myself on my knees and I began to pray to God and plead for America. Then God spoke (not in an audible voice) to my heart as I found myself lying flat on my face on the floor listening to God say these tragic words to me: "**This is not America's second chance, or third, but her *last chance*.**" I want you to know that this was not a dream—this was a calling from God. For the next year and a half (December 2002) under difficult and trying times, God gave me the subject, words, and thoughts to pen into a book. And this is the reason for this message to America.

CHAPTER THREE

The Battle Field

AT TIMES during the course of this message, I have mentioned Christian warfare and the Christian's battle armor. Now, allow me to bring together all that has been said thus far with an easy-to-understand nightmare scenario to illustrate where America is spiritually and morally, and where America is heading. Most Americans can relate to the game of football. It is a game of intense, fast action and emotion, and it is *especially exciting and enjoyable when you are on the winning side.*

Many of you know the game of football is played on a field 100 yards long. One side protects half of the territory and the other team the other half—50 yards apiece. When America started out, she owned and protected the entire playing field—our nation. Our nation was called a Christian nation back then, and everybody knew it, even our young people. Our schools in the beginning stages of America were Christian evangelical schools. More than one hundred colleges and universities started out as Christian schools. Those at the higher level of education were "established primarily for the training of ministers" to do the work of God, such as "Harvard (1636), William and Mary (1693, Anglican); Yale (1701, Congregationalist); Princeton (1746, New Lights Presbyterian); Columbia (1754, Anglican); Brown (1765, Baptist); Rutgers (1766, Dutch Reformed); and Dartmouth (1770, Congregationalist). Dartmouth trained men for missionary work among the Indians."[1]

Engraved in stone at Harvard are these words: "After God had carried us safe to New England and we had built our houses, provided necessaries for our livelihood, rear'd convenient places for God's worship, and settled the civil government: one of the next things we had longed for and looked after was to advance learning and perpetuate it to posterity; dreading to leave an illiterate ministry to the churches, when our present ministers shall lie in the dust."[2]

From that beginning to our present day, *America has lost ground—spiritual and moral yardage—as* we have allowed Satan and his team to take the field of play. *This was the beginning of* **The Battle for America**—the forces of Satan against the forces of God, battling for the minds of America. Satan is going all out to win this battle because of who we are and on what we believe. But tragically, most of the professing Christians are asleep, oblivious to what is taking place. Satan has blinded the minds of backsliding Christians by attacking us with the things of this world—the footmen in our lives. Thus, we are saturated with wealth, comfort, pleasures, entertainment, and sex in order to distract us from what is really taking place—Satan's takeover of America from within and without our land. *Those who are given over to our satanic world systems are not in a battle and*

The Battle Field

see no conflict going on inwardly or outwardly. May God have mercy on us!

Picture the battle for America being played out across this great land of ours—God's team versus Satan's team. **Dear friend, it is a contest of life or death for America.** Most people know that the teams who play on the field are few compared to all the "fans" in the stands. And that is the way it is when it comes down to putting everything on the line for God and country; just a few are on the playing field of battle when it comes to Christian principles and moral standards.

I want to revisit a percentage that was previously mentioned to emphasize how critical our situation is in America. I said that a poll as reported by SRN news on Christian radio, a reliable news source, indicated that 51 percent of Americans "approved" of the so-called homosexual and lesbian lifestyle. If most of the 51 percent are tolerating instead of approving, then this means that they are one step away from acceptance! I see the 51 percent as being the fans who were on God's side once, but switched sides to support Satan's team.

Again, to make matters worse, some states may have passed the non-discrimination hate crimes bill protecting homosexuals and opening the door to possibly giving them the same rights as our God-instituted families. They are now going after legalizing same-sex marriage for every state. If the Church and the conservative people do not rise up and take a stand, and speak out *now,* then our nation will soon be destroyed, because *the foundation of America is God's family structure!* The game will be over for America—Satan will have won!!

Dear friend, these figures are unbelievable and devastating. Most of the churches in America have been silent for many years—not speaking out or taking a stand against these sins. Consequently, these sins have now turned into giant horses, which are now taking charge offensively. We should have every reason to believe that this silence is the work of

Satan. We tend to live in our own little comfortable world while Satan bombards us with all his fleshly distractions to keep our minds off our nation's downward moral spiral. As a result, the spirit throughout America is that of non-involvement—complacent, who cares, lukewarm. We have been taking our freedom for granted. *To not be involved is to be fans supporting Satan's team!*

These are the reasons why Satan and his forces (his team) are on the offenseive, and have been for many years. The devil is the quarterback with the ball of unbelief. His offensive front line and team members are the apostate liberal churches, the public school system, colleges and universities with the teaching of atheism, communism, evolution, and humanism. The result is student rebellion, mass murder of students, backslidden Christians, liberal news media, and liberal politicians. His running backs are homosexuals and lesbians, pornographers, abortionists, the ACLU and NEA, adulterers, fornicators, and the Hollywood movie and TV industry that glorifies these abominable sins.

If Satan is in control of 51 percent of America, then that puts his team over the 50-yard line, or on the 49-yard line of "Christian/Moral" America, and heading for the goal line of total victory. We are losing yardage fast—critical Christian moral principles. Does this remind you of the closeness of the 2001 and the 2005 election of Bush/Kerry presidential election—50 percent for President Bush, and nearly 50 percent against President Bush? Do you sense the tragic and critical picture, friends?

I say the following with a heavy heart, and with the fear of God in my heart: It seems that all of our Christian moral team is on the defensive because we have lost our offense. We have allowed the satanic forces in America to de-throne God our Coach, and His Son, Jesus Christ, our Quarterback. As a result, our small but strong defense is used to try to put out this fire and that fire of immorality, and anti-Americanism.

The Battle Field

Billy Graham's daughter was being interviewed on the TV and was asked, "How could God let something like this happen?" Referring to September 11th, Anne Graham Lotz gave a profound and insightful response. She said, **"I believe that God is deeply saddened by this, just as we are, but for years we have been telling God to get out of our schools, to get out of our government and to get out of our lives. And being the gentlemen that He is, I believe that He has calmly backed out. How can we expect God to give us His blessings and His protection if we demand that He leave us alone?"** This statement says it all! Yes, we have allowed Satan to strip us of our offense in taking God, the Bible, and prayer out of our schools, colleges, and universities. Satan replaced our offense with the teachings of atheism, evolution, humanism, and the Eastern religions. *And then, we dare* to cry out to God by singing "God Bless America," on our nation's Capitol steps and across America! *What we need to do first* is to fall on our faces before God in repentance, rid our nation of our wickedness, and then we can sing out to God for His blessings.

In the beginning of America we were called a "Christian nation," with Jesus Christ on the throne in America. God's team players produced a front-line offense of Christian churches, schools, and universities aflame with the Gospel. America had a strong and powerful team—our running backs were pastors, teachers, evangelists, and missionaries. Jesus Christ was our quarterback with the Bible game ball directing the attack using the Ten Commandments and the Gospel fires of great revivals. Satan's team was not able to get past the first yard marker. As a testimony to this truth, all one has to do is look back at our once Christian schools, colleges, and public buildings, monuments such as Lady Liberty in New York harbor, our nation's currency and coins, the songs of America, and our Pledge of Allegiance. You see God everywhere! However, even though God's name is inscribed all over

America, they are now just by-words, meaningless words, especially to our young people. No one gives a second glance to these preserved and precious words. What a tragedy!

Remember when, and most of the older folks do remember, the homosexuals were in their closets in the darkness of their sin, hardly ever mentioned, and no threat to society. But now, they are out of their closets and on public display. And even though they make up about 6 percent of the total population, as mentioned earlier, a certain percentage of the 6 percent are powerful activist running backs, who are impacting our nation. They are using pressure, extortion, and deception to *capture control* of our leaders in politics all the way up to the very top. They are using big businesses, controlling the news media, and the Hollywood entertainment industry. Thus, in just a few years, Satan's team has sustained an evil offensive driving charge of deception down the playing field, and has gained the *affections of 51 percent of our nation's population*. This is the beginning of *major control*.

Remember when abortion was not even heard about, except to save the life of the mother. Now look where we are, mass murder in our nation is at a tragic epidemic level. Forty million unborn human babies have been aborted—murdered, put to death, or executed since the *Roe v. Wade* decision by our courts in 1973. Beloved, this sin is far greater than the six million people murdered in Hitler's Holocaust atrocities. Our once-strong offense is gone. Satan's offense has taken charge of the Hollywood media, religion, many of our churches, public schools, and universities. Our running backs and the revival fires are being put out. All that is left on our Christian team is the defense. There is no offense. It is all defense, with a front line of real born-again churches, born-again Christian talk ministries, and legal ministries. However, there are not enough Christian activists on defense, because Satan's team is moving ahead with very little opposition.

The Battle Field

You say, "I cannot believe this." But I say to you dear friend, "Just keep your seat in the bleachers, if you are even there; keep your eyes covered with shades of fleshy desires and worldly entertainment; stay in your small little world of self and family obligations, which obviously excuses you for not getting involved as a *player!*" So **sleep on** dear friend, and let wickedness *blind you permanently* as the homosexuals, lesbians, abortionists, adulterers, fornicators, pornographers, murderers, unsaved liberals, and anti-Americans take complete control of our precious nation!

America must wake up before it is too late! *This is our last chance!* Rise up, America and take a stand! Lift up the Word of God and run with the footmen and horses *now* before Satan's team reaches the 10- and 5-yard line, or else *it is all over for this nation!*

Why was Sodom and Gomorrah destroyed? It was not because Sodom and Gomorrah overflowed with homosexuals; *it was because God could not find enough righteous men.* He could not find any offense. Had He found **an offense**, He would not have destroyed the cities. **"Righteousness exhalteth a nation: but sin is a reproach to any people"** (Proverbs 14:34).

Revisit Genesis 18. Abraham tried to bargain with the Lord God in verse 24 and said,

> *"By chance there be fifty righteous within the city: wilt thou also destroy and not spare the place for the fifty righteous that are therein?"*

> *"And the Lord said, If I find in Sodom fifty righteous within the city, then I will spare all the place for their sakes"* (verse 26).

Abraham kept on bargaining with the Lord until he got down to ten righteous men, and in verse 32 the Lord said, "I will not destroy it for ten's sake." But the Lord found none except Lot and his family. The Lord took Lot and his wife and two daughters out of the city and burned the cities of Sodom and Gomorrah "with brimstone and fire" (Genesis 19:24). All the homosexuals perished. All were homosexuals or sympathizers.

Our nation is heading toward this end. I believe we are seeing this happening when a well-known "Christian" denomination, businessmen, and politicians are caving in to the pressure of the these activists, and losing their righteous status! This is not just compromise, but surrender. As grievous as the homosexual sin is, God will *not* destroy America if we have a sufficient number of righteous people to make up the hedge, stand in the gap, and run with the footmen and horses. Therefore, these murderers, rapists, homosexuals, lesbians, abortionists, fornicators, adulterers, pornographers, drug users, and sympathizers **better take heed—cease the spread of their wickedness less the righteous be reduced to such a number that God will suddenly without warning rain down destruction on America and those who practice the above-mentioned sins.**

There are those voices that say it was the terrorist's fault that caused the destruction of the towers. That is partly true, but dear friend, our God is a sovereign God; He is omniscient—all knowing; He is omnipresent—everywhere present; and omnipotent—all-powerful. Our God is in complete control, and superintends all of His creation and everything that takes place. He was well aware of what was taking place on September 11th, and even before September 11th. This event did not take God by surprise. If this were not true, He would not be God. He could have prevented what we term a disaster of great magnitude and indeed it was, but why did He not stop it? Allow me to tell you what He did not allow: *God did not allow what could have been a catastrophic nuclear attack on major cities in this nation with hundreds of thousands of people blown into eternity!*

The Battle Field

Remember, God "is long suffering to us-ward, not willing that any should perish but that all should come to repentance" (2 Peter 3:9). However, He allowed wicked nations to destroy Israel in the past for their disobedience, and more recently Hitler's destruction of six million Jews. *So, we must not think that we can escape the wrath of God! No, not for one moment, dear friends, when America is at the top of the list of nations— number ONE in divorce, abortion, and violent crimes.* Think about that! It was the New Year's Eve prior to 1974 that Billy Graham faced the television audience and said, *"There comes a point beyond which no nation, no community, no family, and individual can go without being judged by God. When we reach that point of moral decadence and idolatry, that God 'gives us up.' Nothing is left but terrifying judgment...Our nation was founded on firm moral principles; our forefathers wanted this to be a nation in which God was honored, and we face the imminent danger of being abandoned by Him."*[3]

Friend, this statement was given on the eve of 1974. How much closer are we now to this prophetic statement being fulfilled! **I want to remind you once again that America's sins are not only greater than Sodom and Gomorrah, but are greater than Hitler's six million atrocities, for we have allowed the murder of forty million plus human beings in the name of abortion!** I believe that God's long-suffering may be coming to a close.

Ezekiel 22:30-31 says,

> "And I sought for a man among them, that should make up the hedge, and stand in the gap before me for the land, that I should not destroy it: but I found none. Therefore have I poured out mine indignation upon them; I have consumed them with the fire of my wrath: their own way have I recompensed upon their heads, saith the Lord God."

Make no mistake about it, God allowed the terrorists to hit America where it really hurts. I believe God has already given us a taste of what we can expect from his displeasure with the 9-11 attack.

While we are fighting terrorists without, within are even greater terrorists, spiritual terrorists that I have identified as footmen and horses. *And, while our military troops are fighting a physical war on terrorists without, we here at home need to rise up and take charge of this spiritual battle going on within our nation. Otherwise, our fighting troops and* **our missionaries** *will come back and find their nation destroyed morally from within, and from without, and tyranny reigning!*

My dear friend, notice all the footmen and horses I identified are actively engaged in bringing America down morally, as the deadly terrorists without brought down the Twin Towers. They are *activist* players, and our troops here and overseas are *activist* players. But, we Christians are staying at home not even in the stands watching Satan and his forces of evil destroy America *from within our country!*

Christians, we must be active for our cause—God and country. Jesus is our example: He actively went about doing His Father's will, which ultimately was to die on the cross for the sins of the world. As Jesus *actively* headed for the cross, He *chased* the money changers from the Holy Temple with a whip; He *spoke the truth* to religious leaders who were seeking to kill Him when He said to them, "**Ye are of your father the devil.**"

In the book of Acts, the disciples of Jesus *actively* went about *preaching, teaching, and spreading* the Gospel of the Lord Jesus Christ. And as a result, three thousand *people were saved at one time.* Later, Steven, Peter, and the Apostle Paul were *martyred* for their faith in Christ. They were *active*. Dear friends, *how real is your faith*? We are either active or non-active! The Apostle Paul said in 2 Timothy 2:3-4, "Thou therefore endure hardness as a good soldier of Jesus Christ. No man that warreth entangleth himself with the affairs of this life; that he may please him who hath chosen him to be a soldier."

How does one become a "good soldier of Jesus Christ?" The answer is found by asking another question, which is very important, so listen carefully! How does one become a good football player? One has to be in good physical condition, know the game, and wear the proper protective equipment. For the Christian soldier, the answer is found earlier in this chapter when I gave you Ephesians 6:10-18. God says, **"Be strong in the Lord, and in the power of his might."** That is quite a powerful command. Why is this so important? It is because as soldiers of Christ we will **"be able to stand against the wiles [deceptions] of the devil. For we wrestle not against flesh and blood, but against spiritual wickedness in high places."** This is spiritual warfare, my friend.

How are we to be strong in the Lord and thereby understand Satan's deadly game of deception? 2 Timothy 2:15 says, "Study to show thyself approved of God, a workman that needeth not be ashamed, rightly dividing the word of truth." And "So then faith cometh by hearing, and hearing by the word of God" (Romans 10:17). By faith then we become strong in having "put on the whole armour of God." *This is spiritual armor, which produces spiritual strength.*

What are the pieces of armor? God says, "having your loins girt about with the truth...having on the breastplate of righteousness...feet shod with the preparation of the gospel of peace...shield of faith...helmet of salvation...the sword of the Spirit, which is the word of God...and prayer."

Truth is God's truth, which is absolute truth, the "word of truth" (2 Timothy 2:15). Truth is displayed throughout the Bible. Our young people are being taught that there is no such thing as absolute truth. This is my response to that question:

Are you absolutely sure there are no absolute truths? **"Howbeit when he, the Spirit of truth is come, he will guide you into all truth" (John 16:13)**. The indwelling Spirit of Christ reveals truth to the Christian. I go into detail on truth in chapter 6, "Conclusion." Briefly, the righteousness mentioned here is not our righteousness, but God's righteousness in us. Ours is "filthy rags" (Isaiah 64:6). The shield of faith should be a strong faith in God in order to win battles. Be sure you have the "helmet of salvation"—real salvation, and not religion. Religion does not save anyone, or make one strong **in the Lord**! Only a personal relationship with Jesus Christ makes one strong in the Lord, and thereby becoming *active* for Christ! I describe in detail some of the ways to be active for God and country in chapter 5 titled, "What can we do?"

Dear friend, if we do not **study** the Bible, the sword of the Spirit, then we cannot know our enemy. Therefore, we become a weak and naked spiritual disaster. We will not be able to take a **stand** on anything, thus losing the battle for America, and the game of life or death! Again, when we really study the Bible, our faith becomes strong.

God is looking for those who **"having done all, to stand"** as ACTIVE CHRISTIAN SOLDIERS for the front line of battle. I repeat, we are either on the field of battle (making up the hedge, standing in the gap, running with the footmen and horses), or we are spiritually out-of-shape Christians (warming the church pew, staying at home watching TV), or way out in the stands of society (weighted down with sin, and **"entangled with the affairs of this life"**) away from the critical condition of America—the battlefield. **Dear friends, where are you? This is more than a football game; this is a battle of life or death for America! This is our last chance, our last hour—the clock is ticking its last ticks!**

We must at all cost regain the offence we have lost to Satan by defensively turning back the forces of Satan NOW;

The Battle Field

otherwise, we will have lost the battle for life. **Wake up America!** May Jesus Christ resurrect the sleeping church of America and lead us to victory across our great land. May God help us and have mercy on us, and remove the blinds of darkness from our spiritual eyes.

CHAPTER FOUR

Some Final Words

LET US READ again the text from the Word of God—it cannot be emphasized enough. Let it be part of your thinking and respond.

> "If thou hast run with the footmen, and they have wearied thee, then how canst thou contend with the horses? And if in the land of peace, wherein thou trustedst, they wearied thee, then how wilt thou do in the swelling of Jordan?" (Jeremiah 12:5)

> "And I sought for a man among them, that should make up the hedge, and stand in the gap before me for the land, that I should not destroy it: but I found none. Therefore have I poured out mine indignation upon them; I have consumed them with the fire of my

wrath: their own way have I recompensed upon their heads, saith the Lord God" (Ezekiel 22:30-31).

"The wicked shall be turned into hell, and all nations that forget God" (Psalm 9:17).

Jesus Christ said these words in Luke 12:48, "**For unto whomsoever much is given, of him shall be much required.**" A few pages ago I mentioned our nation's Capitol, but do you know what is atop the Capitol? Multitudes have no idea. "High atop the United States Capitol dome in Washington DC stands the statue of a stately Freedom Lady, almost twenty feet high. Her face is framed by a crest of stars. A shield of stars and stripes is in her right hand, symbolizing our flag of freedom. A sheathed sword is under her right hand, suggesting that while our independence has been won, the sword is ready for use whenever needed to preserve our freedoms. The sculptured Freedom Lady was brought from Rome during the Civil War. On the ocean her ship encountered a fierce storm and the captain ordered some cargo thrown overboard. The sailors wanted to include the heavy statue, but the captain refused, shouting above the wind, "No, Never! We'll flounder before we throw 'Freedom' away."[1]

Yes, our freedom is very precious, but the tragedy is that we do not realize what we have taken for granted all these years until we lose it. *To this present generation of Americans I say, "Let us not be responsible for causing thousands of men and women from the beginning of this great nation to the present to die in vain fighting to defend our freedom. Rise up, Americans, and stand in the gap for God, His nation, and our freedom!"* "**If God be for us, who can be against us?**" (Romans 8:31).

Dear friend, God has given **much to America**, and now He is saying to America today, to us, that **much shall be required to protect our freedom.** Think about this: If we

Some Final Words

cannot run with the spiritual terrorist footmen and horses within our nation and get the victory, how can we expect God to give us the victory over the terrorist nations who are poised to strike us again from without, and *from within*! Dear friends, can you not see our liberty slipping away at a rapid pace? And, if we continue living as if there is no God, we are going to lose what we take for granted—our precious freedom. Freedom is not free; it has a high price tag. Unless God intervenes, and unless we as a nation humble ourselves before God in repentance, I can see possibly within the next five to ten years losing our freedom, our nation, and *the true Christian Church of America* going underground because of unparalleled persecution. *Yes*, I am talking about America. May God help us to obey our Creator and Savior. Turn from our sin to God; stand in the gap (occupy), make up the hedge of righteousness for America, run with the footmen and horses to victory for the cause of Christ and America, Amen!

CHAPTER FIVE

What Can We Do? (An Offense Plan)

IF YOU CLAIM to be a Christian, then I strongly encourage you to *get involved.* A soldier is *actively involved.* The following action list will help us all to take a stand, and get us running for God and country:

1. 2 Chronicles 7:14 "If my people which are called by my name, shall humble themselves, and pray, and seek my face, and turn from their wicked ways: then will I hear from heaven, and forgive their sins, and heal their land."

The first thing we need to do as Christian Americans is to fall to our knees before God Almighty and confess our sins, repent of our sins (turn from our sins to God), and ask Him to forgive us. We *must* mean what we pray, or God will not hear our prayers. *This is the most important beginning step for anyone who wants to mean business for God. Without this beginning step, we are wasting our time. We will not get involved. There must be a God-sent Holy Ghost revival in America. It begins with the church members.* Because of the condition of the Church and the people of America as I have described above, our land needs a healing touch from God, but the backslidden Christians do not know it—"They that are whole have no need of the physician" (Mark 2:17). The Holy Spirit was sent into the world and lives within the believing heart of Christians, the Church, to convict the unsaved of sin. But Christians have become so much a part of this satanic world system that it is hard to tell who is spiritually dead or alive. America needs a healing touch from Jesus Christ, the Great Physician. It is up to the Church to occupy God's America. Dear God, revive the Church, lest we be destroyed!

2. Set aside some time to *pray* and *study* your Bible at home on your own (Acts 6:4; 2 Timothy 2:15). This is a *must*. *Do both daily, another must. Begin the day by praying.* Once this is put into practice, you will find yourself walking with God, possessing the mind of Christ, and your life will be changing before your very eyes. Your day will be different. When you pray, pray first for yourself, and get right with God; otherwise, He will not hear your prayers. This is very important and cannot be over emphasized. Then, pray for your family, lost loved ones, and friends, your neighbors, people you know at work, and those at work who are lost without Christ. Pray for your church family, your church leaders, missionaries, and churches across the nation. Pray for our public school system, colleges, and universities. Then pray for our nation, our president and other leaders, Christian organizations, former Supreme Court Judge Roy Moore of Alabama and other appointees, and others who are standing in the gap for Christ and country. Pray for the groups of people mentioned in this book, who are out to destroy our nation. These

suggestions are just to get you started. I am sure the Holy Spirit will bring others to mind as you start praying and become a prayer warrior. I believe with all my heart that a remnant of godly prayer warriors praying daily for America is one of the reasons why God has spared America thus far.

3. Give at least a tenth of your **gross** income, the tithe, to the Lord at your local church (Genesis 28:22; Malachi 3:8; 1 Corinthians 16:1-2). Be sure *you are in* a born-again, Bible-believing church in which the people love the Lord, where souls are being saved regularly, where *all your tithe* goes to the work of the Lord at that church, where they preach the whole council of God, and definitely takes a stand on the above issues (Hebrews 10: 25; Acts 2:47). If your pastor never mentions any of the above sins I previously covered, then I would question your pastor on where he stands on these issues.

Give over and above the tenth as the Lord gives the increase. We should not hold back on our giving to the Lord, for we cannot out-give the Lord (Luke 6:38). Give the first tenth of increase to the Lord through the local church; then from that same increase, give monthly support to missionaries from your church, or ones you know personally.

Over and above your local church tithe, support financially other Bible-believing Christian organizations that are making up the hedge, standing in the gap, and running with the footmen and horses. I can name a number of good organizations that I support, which are out there actively taking a stand on these issues without compromise. Some of these I have mentioned above in this book. Support the Boys Scouts of America in any way you can, and pray for them.

4. Be faithful in taking your entire family to church Sunday morning, Sunday night, Wednesday night, and any other services, such as missionary conferences, and evangelistic

meetings. Get involved in your church serving the Lord as the Lord leads you and opens doors. Faithfully have family devotions with your children.

5. Listen to Christian radio and Christian news. Keep abreast of what is going on, for Christian radio news gives secular, Christian, and conservative views—something that the main news media seldom mentions. God is looking for those who will buy radio stations across America for new Christian stations without the satanic contemporary "rock music." This is very important. Take this window of opportunity before it is too late!

6. Write the president about these issues. Insist that he take a stand and speak out against immorality and anti-Americanism. Insist that the president stop all support, including financial support, of the United Nations (UN), which is developing into a one-world government and police state. We must not allow our troops to become part of the UN. We must maintain our sovereignty at all cost. Thank the president for doing a good job. Write your senators and congressmen on where you stand on these issues. Let them know that we are not going to continue to allow such gross immorality.

7. Let your voice be heard. Get involved! Start in your local community. Share this book with others, and give copies out to those you know are lost, and Christian friends. Parents and all true Americans, join together and let your voice be heard. *Begin writing letters to* the NEA, the ACLU, and the public schools and libraries. Insist that the abominable pornography, promotion of homosexuality, atheistic teachings of evolution and humanism, including the indoctrination of the false gods of religion be obliterated from our public schools, colleges, universities, and public libraries.

What Can We Do? (An Offense Plan)

Insist that God and His Word, the Bible, be put back in our public schools and universities like in the beginning of this great nation of God.

8. Flood our president, congressmen and senators with letters insisting the same. Do not be weak-minded and be destroyed. Our weakness and unconcern has allowed sin to blossom. Now is the time to say enough is enough! May God help us to do it; and He will, the moment you take that first step! Our God is waiting—what are you going to do, America?

9. Vote in primary and national elections. This is tremendously important. I cannot over-emphasize this enough. If all the professing Christians voted each year, I do not believe our nation would be in such a saddened state. Out of the millions of professing Christians in America, only a fraction of them vote. If all of the professing Christians voted, it would have been a landslide in the 2001 and 2005 presidential elections, instead of almost 50-50. What a tragedy we do not stand up for what we believe. The devil's crowd makes a statement. **Voting now and in the future is for the moral survival of our nation, beloved!** Vote out of office those in the leadership locally and of our nation that do not take a Christian stand, or at least a conservative stand on the moral issues above. Vote in those who do. Christians, it is your duty! God says, "Occupy till I come" (Luke 19:13). *Remember, it was God Who gave birth to this nation using Christian leadership.* Dear friend, to not vote is an "I do not care vote," or a vote for evil. Therefore, use your God-given gifts and your God-given opportunities while we still have them; one is to vote, and another is to get involved in the political arena of our nation like some have and are making a difference. You see, God raises up leaders, and it is *your vote* God uses to put in office the right persons and the right party.

A word of caution! While you may be voting for the right individual, the party's platform may be promoting immoral and wrong causes. If we do not understand what is going on, or we do not bother to vote, then Satan's workers will occupy as we have experienced in the past, and as we are now experiencing.

10. While we are doing the above, I strongly recommend that you begin to take your children out of the public schools, and enroll them in Christian schools, or homeschool your children regardless of the status of your situation. You can do it. Thousands of Christian schools are being raised up as well as homeschools. Our God will supply your needs for this. He is waiting for us to step up. There is a lot of information out there on how to start a homeschool. Anyone can do it. It is very, very affordable.

God's Word says, "Train up a child in the way he should go: and when he is old, he will not depart from it" (Proverbs 22:6). Dear parents, this means God's "way." "Bring them up in the nurture and admonition of the Lord" (Ephesians 6:4). I believe the "way" the public school system is now training our children is the very opposite of God's "way!" May God richly bless you as you begin to make up the hedge, stand in the gap, and run with the footmen and horses with the Word of God and get the victory!

CHAPTER SIX

Conclusion

I TRUST that you have been with me to this point, and taken thought of where you are spirtually in your life. And I trust the message of this book has impacted your life to take action and to be part of the hedge for God and our nation. May God help you to be a part in winning America back to God!

Some of you may be concerned about your spiritual life, or maybe you have been pretending to be a Christian, and God's Holy Spirit has spoken to you about sin in your life. Maybe you are a religious person, a church member, or maybe you never go to church. Perhaps you have never heard words like this before, but God is speaking to you and your heart is disturbed. And maybe you are questioning everything that was said, so please, dear friend, read on if you value the destiny of your soul.

Maybe you have read this message and the Lord is dealing with you about your relationship with another person, and you know now that it is wrong. The Holy Spirit has convicted you of this involvement, and you need some help. It is the work of the Holy Spirit to convict and convince us of sin and our need to respond to God's voice immediately. If you have never trusted Christ as your Lord and Savior, then now is the time to do it. Remember God's love is no respecter of persons, and **God loves us regardless of our *behavior* and is waiting with open arms to forgive, and save us from our sins.**

For those of you who may still be thinking, "I just do not believe all that because what may be right for you is not right for me. Also, there are many cultures and religions such as Hinduism, Islam, Buddhism, Shinto, etc, and the 'culture of America' is just one of many. Therefore, what may be right for you and our culture may not be right for me, or their culture. In other words there is no actual right or wrong, for everything is relative." Really? Does this kind of thinking sound logical? Think about that, friend: *This is the kind of teaching that is being taught to our young people today in our schools, colleges, and universities.* **With this kind of thinking, responsibility and accountability are eliminated from society, thereby allowing society members to do their own thing regardless of how it affects others.** This is what we have allowed to be taught to our children and young people by these scholarly teachers and professors. How long is our nation going to tolerate this kind of mind control? This is not something new; we are experiencing a repeat of the same thing that happened thousands of years ago.

In the book of Judges we find Israel "doing their own thing" and suffering the consequences time after time. At the end of the book, the final words are these: "**Every man did that which was right in his own eyes**" (Judges 21:25). On the other hand, "There is a way which seemeth right unto man, but the end thereof are the ways of death" (Proverbs 14:12). And Jesus said, "I am the way, the truth, and the life, no man cometh unto the Father, but by me" (John 14:6).

Listen carefully! I trust you will be able to understand that this kind of thinking is not logical and causes one to be dangerously misdirected in life, resulting in utter confusion, chaos, and death. If you think really hard, you will discover that almost everything we do in this life has instructions, regulations, and rules to follow *in order to do the right thing and live together as a society.* There is a right way and a wrong way to do things. For example, before we can drive a car, we must be more than familiar with the *book of instructions* that comes with the car in order to find out how it operates for our own good as well as others. Otherwise, as most of us have found out the hard way, it costs us dearly. So we must learn all about the car and how to take good care of it, or pay the penalty.

Now, do you do your own thing about your car, or do you follow the instructions on what to do, or not to do? If you are smart, you will obey the instructions and not say, "Well, that may be the right way to do that in order for you to operate the car, but not right for me." How foolish, you would think? Let us say you do the right thing; follow the directions and not mess up your car. Now that we are familiar with our car, are we ready to drive in traffic? The answer is NO. Before we can drive on the road in traffic, we need another book of instructions: *traffic laws, rules and regulations.*

Believe me, dear friend, *we had better be more than just familiar with these traffic laws and rules, or it can be very costly for us.* In order to get a driver's license and drive the car, one must pass the tests—both the written and the road tests. When we disobey the traffic signal light and go through it when it is red, we pay a penalty called a "fine" plus points on our driving record. This is called *breaking the traffic laws,* and therefore *we have to pay a price for our transgression, and in a lot of cases the penalty is very costly.* For most of us, when we see these laws displayed out there in traffic, whether it is a stop sign or traffic light, *we automatically obey them.* We do not argue with these laws; we accept them for our protection as well as others. What if there were no traffic laws! There would be total chaos, not to mention multitudes of deaths, accidents, and injuries. Society would not survive.

Notice one thing about these laws: these laws do not distinguish between cultures. They transcend cultures. It does not matter where you are from, or your background culture and your religion. We have traffic laws that *all individuals must obey.* So, why do all the "cultures" in *America* obey these laws? Why do you obey a stop sign, traffic light, or speed signs? Your answer should include: "It is *right for me* to obey these laws, just as it is *wrong for me* not to obey these laws, because I do not want to get hurt, killed, or possibly injure or kill someone else! And, I do not want my driver's license taken from me, etc." Where is your relativism here? Where is your culture here? Where is your religion here? All of these do not apply—*we are all on common ground with the traffic laws of society*

Likewise, *it is the same when it comes to the spiritual and moral laws of the societies of God's created world!* I suggest that you allow your mind to apply the simple truths of the traffic laws of society to the spiritual and moral laws for all cultures of this world—one great mass of people all over this globe. Jehovah God is the living and **loving** Creator of ***all* people on this entire planet Earth.** He does not confine Himself to a portion of the world called America, or this culture or that culture, "God so loved the world" (John 3:16). The word *world* refers to mankind. God has so much love for us that He has written a B*ook of Instructions* in the right way and the wrong way for His worldwide creation. He has given illustrations of both cases, transcending all cultures and all religions, to instruct His creation on how to live as individuals, as a society, as a nation, and how to prepare oneself for eternity.

Just as there are traffic laws to keep society from destroying itself, there are laws, rules, and regulations from God, our loving Creator, to tell us how to live with one another in His societies of His world. The reason why is obvious: so that we do not end up destroying one another, societies and nations. Some of these laws from God are moral, and they are just and right.

God says that if we break His laws, **and all of His creation has**, there is a price to be paid, and that is death. Romans 3:23 says, "For *all* have sinned and come short of the glory of God." And, "The wages of sin is death" (Romans 6:23). Again, God also says, "Whatsoever we sow, we shall reap." This means good or bad; we will reap what we sow! The Ten Commandments are like a gigantic stop sign, and are examples of God's basic laws *for individuals, nations, and cultures to show us that we are sinners*. We all have failed to stop, and God says we are transgressors of His laws. There are no exceptions, for we are all in the process of dying as proof that **God's Word is true**, *and it is because we have sinned against our God*.

The sins I called "footmen and horses" are from God, not from me. You can argue with me, but you cannot argue with **God**! They are **His laws**, not mine. Do we argue with those who set up our traffic laws? No, we accept them and respect them by obeying them. It is totally unacceptable with God for His creation to say to Him, "That may be right for you, but not for me." Can you not see how ridiculous that sounds? Therefore, we are without excuse, for all people are on common ground in God's eyes. Think about that! Therefore, we should not try to explain away what God has written; we should believe Him and respect His laws just like our traffic laws. After all, He created us and knows what is best for us, and He expects us to obey His laws. This is the only way to live and display RESPECT and LOVE *for each other in our society*. This is God's way of controlling His people and society, just like our traffic laws. What God says is sin, is sin, and we had better believe Him.

The only way we can please God is to agree with Him and allow Him to take charge of our lives. It is not easy to do what I just said because Satan deceives, and spiritually blinds us to the truth in order to keep all of us slaves to our sin nature and to him. Satan will try to convince you to continue to live in unbelief and do your thing. But, I hasten to say that it will be your unbelief that will take you to that awful place called hell that God has prepared for all those who choose to remain in unbelief.

Hell is a real place of conscious existence in an eternity of torment without God (Luke 16:19-31). However, *if you choose to say no to Satan, then here are the steps to eternal forgiveness and eternal life with God in heaven*:

Realize you are a sinner in God's sight and cannot save yourself (Romans 3:23). You have sinned against a holy and righteous God by breaking His laws.

Believe that God loves you in spite of your sin. He has demonstrated His love for you by allowing His only begotten Son, Jesus Christ, the sinless one, to take your sin on Himself, and to die in your place on the cross to pay your sin debt (Romans 5:8).

Believe that Jesus Christ rose from the grave, and is seated at the right hand of the Father in heaven waiting to forgive you of your sins (Romans 10:9, 1 Corinthians 15:3-4, 2 Peter 3:9). There is no sin so great or destructive, even if you are at the point of thinking there is nothing left but to take your own life, that God cannot forgive completely and restore, and make your life beautiful in His eyes.

Conclusion

Listen to these inspired words of this beautiful chorus, "Something beautiful, something good; All my confusion He understood; All I had to offer Him was broken-ness and strife, But He made something beautiful of my life."[1]

And, when God does that in you, then you will be singing another beautiful new song like this called "**My Tribute**" "How can I say thanks for the things You have done for me—things so undeserved, yet You give to prove Your love for me. The voices of a million angels could not express my gratitude—All that I am and ever hope to be, I owe it all to Thee. To God be the glory, To God be the glory; to God be the glory for the things He has done. With His blood He has saved me; With His power He has raised me; To God be the glory for the things He has done. Just let me live my life; Let it be pleasing, Lord, to Thee. And should I gain any praise, let it go to Calvary. With His blood He has saved me; With His power He has raised me; To God be the glory for the things He has done."[2]

Dear friend, Christ can do that for you! He paid your sin debt in full for you. Jesus Christ satisfied the holiness of God the Father's righteous demands when He became our perfect sacrifice—**our sin bearer for all people.** God now has a basis on which to offer as a gift forgiveness, salvation, and eternal peace with Him. And when Jesus Christ rose from the grave, that assures us of eternal forgiveness and eternal life with God *forever* to all those who will repent of their sin of unbelief.

Luke 13:3 says, "Except ye repent, ye shall all likewise perish." We have a great and loving God! To repent means to turn from our sin, our sinful way of living, to Christ, and receive Him by faith into our heart as Lord and Savior. John 1:12 says, "But as many as received him, to them gave he the power to become the sons of God, even to them that believe on his name." And, "whosoever shall call upon the name of the Lord shall be saved" (Romans 10:13).

4. If you believe the above with all your heart, then bow before God and pray a simple prayer like this: *"Dear Lord Jesus, I repent of my sin of unbelief. I believe You died on the cross for my sin, and rose from the dead. I am sorry I sinned against You. I turn from my sin to You, and ask You to forgive me, and come into my heart and save me now."* If you truly mean it, Jesus will absolutely honor your request, save you, and give you assurance of your salvation.

When you have invited Jesus Christ to come into your heart and life and really meant it, Christ's Spirit actually enters within your soul—your innermost being, and saves you. He gives you a new heart, a new nature, a new life in Christ's love, and a new beginning. 2 Corinthians 5:17 says, **"Therefore if any man be in Christ, he is a new creature: old things are passed away; behold, all things are become new."** It is the Spirit of Christ Who lives within your heart, Who gives you the power to over-come your sin nature and Satan, and Who enables you to do right instead of wrong. For you have the very person within you Who gave us His commandments and enables you with His power to be obedient to His commandments or laws because of His love shed abroad in your heart. That's grace, friend, God's grace. You have the very life of God within you—eternal life!

I just want to repeat this again, because I just love to say that you possess a new nature from God. This gives you great **power** and **victory** over your old sin nature, and you are able to please Him. T*ruly, if you have experienced salvation, you are actually "born again" (John 3:3-7) spiritually from above. You possess God's life, eternal life. You will see life differently;* ***you will know what is right and what is wrong, for you now have been given spiritual eyes from God to begin to see things as God sees them.*** You become a child of God! This is a relationship of love with our Creator, God—not a religion. This is the only way there can be true peace and love for all peoples of all nations.

Conclusion

My prayer is that God will help you to understand these great and wonderful spiritual truths and respond. If you have not already, respond to the Word of God and invite Jesus Christ into your heart and life at this very moment. *All we have to do is to take that step of faith toward God, and He will be with you, and in you forever. That is a promise from God,* "**I will never leave you nor forsake you**" (**Hebrews 13:5**). *May God help you to respond!* Thank you for reading this book, and I trust it has helped you. Pass it on to your friend or relative, and may God bless you.

SOURCE REFERENCES

Chapter 1
1. Peter Marshall and David Manuel, *The Light and the Glory* (Old Tappan, New Jersey: Fleming H. Revell Company, 1977), pp 31, 41.
2. Reprinted from *Annals of America* © 1968, 1976, Encyclopedia Britannica, Inc. Vol 1 pp 4-5.
3. Ibid. p 64.
4. James C. Hefley, *One Nation Under God*, (Victor Books, 1975), p 14.
5. Ibid. pp 16, 34.
6. Ibid. pp 16-17.
7. Peter Marshall and David Manuel, *The Light and the Glory* (Old Tappan, New Jersey: Fleming H. Revell Company, 1977), p. 343.
8. James C. Hefley, *One Nation Under God* (Victor Books, 1975), pp 10-11.
9. Ibid. p. 125.
10. Ibid. p. 128.
11. Various sources—This statement has been attributed to Alexis de Tocqueville but cannot be verified for it does not appear in his writings.

Chapter 2
1. Some contributing factors that *may encourage* homosexual behavior: (the Bible does not deal with why people are attracted toward this behavior, but deals with the act itself, the behavior, which God calls sin). Briefly, the aspect of why a lot of homosexuals become homosexuals is based upon studies indicating a "gender identity problem"—a masculine identity, which is dependent upon the father and son relationship. The son must see in his father his masculinity, his strength, his affections, and his leadership in the home. The son must look up to his father, and there must be a favorable relationship between the father, son, and mother. The father must spend time with his son, not with the TV, and not the reverse—the son spending most of his time with his mother, and the TV. And if there is no father, as is the case with multitudes of families, the son is spending all his time with motherly affections, and or sister affections. And this is

the making of a "gender confusion" situation early on in the young life of the boy. As a result, the son looks for masculinity and love from a man. But he doesn't find the masculine kind of love in a homosexual relationship, because in a lot of cases, his partner has the same problem—gender identity and masculine affections when there isn't any such affection available. As a result, there will not be any lasting relationship with one another. Therefore, one can understand that this kind of upbringing *may encourage* one toward unnatural behavior in order to compensate for what was lacking in the family environment. But, it is still a matter of *choice*: the son *chooses* to look for masculine affections from another man, and by experimenting in the sin, finds it pleasurable. Still others have been molested by homosexuals—forced to submit, but after a time find the sin pleasurable, and by *choice* they continue in the sin. The same is true for those who are looking for attention, and by *choice* they experiment and continue in the homosexual sin. One can "enjoy the pleasures of sin," *but only* "for a season" (Hebrews 11:25). For more information on the subject of "gender identity confusion," the author highly recommends a Web site, www.narth.com

2. Center for Reclaiming America FASTFACTS articles, "Seven DEMANDS of the Homosexual Agenda: Set forth and distributed at the 'Gay Pride' March on Washington, DC, April 25, 1993."

3. *Washington Post* newspaper, November 14, 1999.

4. Family Research Council, "Seven Fallacies Behind 'Project 10' by Joseph Nicolosi, Ph.D. Used by permission.

5. John and Anne Paulk, *Love Won Out* (Tyndale House); Tape, "Re-igniting the Hope for Homosexuals."

6. "Baby Parts" video, *Point of View* radio talk program.

7. Ibid.

8. The National Marriage Project Publication "Should We Live Together?" by David Popenoe, Ph.D., and Barbara Dafoe Whitehead, Ph.D., Second Edition, Rutgers, The University Of New Jersey), pp. 3-4. Used by permission.

9. Ibid.

10. Ibid.

11. From Break Point, Dec. 21, 2004, reprinted with permission of Prison Fellowship, www.breakpoint.org.

12. From "Grading the NEA: A Special Report" published by Focus on the Family. Copyright © 2001, Focus on the Family. All rights reserved. International copyright secured. Used by permission.

13. "Statue of Liberty" Words and music by Neil Enloe. Used by permission.

Source References

14. Used by permission of Good News Publishers, 1300 Cresent Street, Wheaton, IL 60187 USA.
15. Ibid.
16. Ibid.
17. Recorded on tape.
18. Used by permission of Good News Publishers, 1300 Cresent Street, Wheaton, IL 60187 USA.

Chapter 3
1. James C. Hefley, *One Nation Under God* (Victor Books, 1975), p. 78.
2. Reprinted from *Annals of America* © 1968, 1976, Encyclopedia Britannica, Inc. Vol 1. pp 175.
3. James C. Hefley, *One Nation Under God* (Victor Books, 1975), p. 6.

Chapter 4
1. James C. Hefley, *One Nation Under God*, (Victor Books, 1975), p. 35.

Chapter 6
1. "Something Beautiful" Words by Gloria Gaither. Music by William J. Gaither. Copyright © 1971 William J. Gaither, Inc. All rights controlled by Gaither Copyright Management. Used by permission.
2. "My Tribute" ©Bud John Songs, INC. Words and Music by Andraé Crouch. All rights reserved. Used by permission.

The Battle for America
Order Form

Postal orders: 13610 Broadfording Church Rd.
Hagerstown, MD 21740

Telephone orders: 301-791-6423

E-mail orders: pdonley7@aol.com

Please send *The Battle for America* **to:**

Name: _____

Address: _____

City: _____ State: _____

Zip: _____ Telephone: (_____) _____

Book Price: $10.95

Shipping: $3.00 for the first book and $1.00 for each additional book to cover shipping and handling within US, Canada, and Mexico. International orders add $6.00 for the first book and $2.00 for each additional book.

Or order from:
ACW Press
1200 HWY 231 South #273
Ozark, AL 36360

(800) 931-BOOK

or contact your local bookstore

Basic DNA and RNA Protocols

Methods in Molecular Biology™
John M. Walker, SERIES EDITOR

60. **Protein NMR Protocols,** edited by *David G. Reid, 1996*
59. **Protein Purification Protocols,** edited by *Shawn Doonan, 1996*
58. **Basic DNA and RNA Protocols,** edited by *Adrian J. Harwood, 1996*
57. **In Vitro Mutagenesis Protocols,** edited by *Michael K. Trower, 1996*
56. **Crystallographic Methods and Protocols,** edited by *Christopher Jones, Barbara Mulloy, and Mark Sanderson, 1996*
55. **Plant Cell Electroporation and Electrofusion Protocols,** edited by *Jac A. Nickoloff, 1995*
54. **YAC Protocols,** edited by *David Markie, 1995*
53. **Yeast Protocols:** *Methods in Cell and Molecular Biology,* edited by *Ivor H. Evans, 1996*
52. **Capillary Electrophoresis:** *Principles, Instrumentation, and Applications,* edited by *Kevin D. Altria, 1996*
51. **Antibody Engineering Protocols,** edited by *Sudhir Paul, 1995*
50. **Species Diagnostics Protocols:** *PCR and Other Nucleic Acid Methods,* edited by *Justin P. Clapp, 1996*
49. **Plant Gene Transfer and Expression Protocols,** edited by *Heddwyn Jones, 1995*
48. **Animal Cell Electroporation and Electrofusion Protocols,** edited by *Jac A. Nickoloff, 1995*
47. **Electroporation Protocols for Microorganisms,** edited by *Jac A. Nickoloff, 1995*
46. **Diagnostic Bacteriology Protocols,** edited by *Jenny Howard and David M. Whitcombe, 1995*
45. **Monoclonal Antibody Protocols,** edited by *William C. Davis, 1995*
44. ***Agrobacterium* Protocols,** edited by *Kevan M. A. Gartland and Michael R. Davey, 1995*
43. **In Vitro Toxicity Testing Protocols,** edited by *Sheila O'Hare and Chris K. Atterwill, 1995*
42. **ELISA:** *Theory and Practice,* by *John R. Crowther, 1995*
41. **Signal Transduction Protocols,** edited by *David A. Kendall and Stephen J. Hill, 1995*
40. **Protein Stability and Folding:** *Theory and Practice,* edited by *Bret A. Shirley, 1995*
39. **Baculovirus Expression Protocols,** edited by *Christopher D. Richardson, 1995*
38. **Cryopreservation and Freeze-Drying Protocols,** edited by *John G. Day and Mark R. McLellan, 1995*
37. **In Vitro Transcription and Translation Protocols,** edited by *Martin J. Tymms, 1995*
36. **Peptide Analysis Protocols,** edited by *Ben M. Dunn and Michael W. Pennington, 1994*
35. **Peptide Synthesis Protocols,** edited by *Michael W. Pennington and Ben M. Dunn, 1994*
34. **Immunocytochemical Methods and Protocols,** edited by *Lorette C. Javois, 1994*
33. ***In Situ* Hybridization Protocols,** edited by *K. H. Andy Choo, 1994*
32. **Basic Protein and Peptide Protocols,** edited by *John M. Walker, 1994*
31. **Protocols for Gene Analysis,** edited by *Adrian J. Harwood, 1994*
30. **DNA–Protein Interactions,** edited by *G. Geoff Kneale, 1994*
29. **Chromosome Analysis Protocols,** edited by *John R. Gosden, 1994*
28. **Protocols for Nucleic Acid Analysis by Nonradioactive Probes,** edited by *Peter G. Isaac, 1994*
27. **Biomembrane Protocols:** *II. Architecture and Function,* edited by *John M. Graham and Joan A. Higgins, 1994*
26. **Protocols for Oligonucleotide Conjugates:** *Synthesis and Analytical Techniques,* edited by *Sudhir Agrawal, 1994*
25. **Computer Analysis of Sequence Data:** *Part II,* edited by *Annette M. Griffin and Hugh G. Griffin, 1994*
24. **Computer Analysis of Sequence Data:** *Part I,* edited by *Annette M. Griffin and Hugh G. Griffin, 1994*
23. **DNA Sequencing Protocols,** edited by *Hugh G. Griffin and Annette M. Griffin, 1993*
22. **Microscopy, Optical Spectroscopy, and Macroscopic Techniques,** edited by *Christopher Jones, Barbara Mulloy, and Adrian H. Thomas, 1993*
21. **Protocols in Molecular Parasitology,** edited by *John E. Hyde, 1993*
20. **Protocols for Oligonucleotides and Analogs:** *Synthesis and Properties,* edited by *Sudhir Agrawal, 1993*
19. **Biomembrane Protocols:** *I. Isolation and Analysis,* edited by *John M. Graham and Joan A. Higgins, 1993*
18. **Transgenesis Techniques:** *Principles and Protocols,* edited by *David Murphy and David A. Carter, 1993*
17. **Spectroscopic Methods and Analyses:** *NMR, Mass Spectrometry, and Metalloprotein Techniques,* edited by *Christopher Jones, Barbara Mulloy, and Adrian H. Thomas, 1993*
16. **Enzymes of Molecular Biology,** edited by *Michael M. Burrell, 1993*
15. **PCR Protocols:** *Current Methods and Applications,* edited by *Bruce A. White, 1993*
14. **Glycoprotein Analysis in Biomedicine,** edited by *Elizabeth F. Hounsell, 1993*
13. **Protocols in Molecular Neurobiology,** edited by *Alan Longstaff and Patricia Revest, 1992*
12. **Pulsed-Field Gel Electrophoresis:** *Protocols, Methods, and Theories,* edited by *Margit Burmeister and Levy Ulanovsky, 1992*
11. **Practical Protein Chromatography,** edited by *Andrew Kenney and Susan Fowell, 1992*
10. **Immunochemical Protocols,** edited by *Margaret M. Manson, 1992*
9. **Protocols in Human Molecular Genetics,** edited by *Christopher G. Mathew, 1991*
8. **Practical Molecular Virology:** *Viral Vectors for Gene Expression,* edited by *Mary K. L. Collins, 1991*
7. **Gene Transfer and Expression Protocols,** edited by *Edward J. Murray, 1991*
6. **Plant Cell and Tissue Culture,** edited by *Jeffrey W. Pollard and John M. Walker, 1990*
5. **Animal Cell Culture,** edited by *Jeffrey W. Pollard and John M. Walker, 1990*